GOD PRINT

MAKING YOUR MARK FOR CHRIST

SKIP H

D1466634

BRIDGE
LOGOS
FOUNDATION

Alachua, Florida 32615

Bridge-Logos
Alachua, FL 32615 USA

Godprint
Making Your Mark for Christ
by Skip Heitzig

Printed in the United States of America.

Library of Congress Catalog Card Number: 2009943801
International Standard Book Number 978-0-88270-631-3

Cover design: Brandi Heft

Photograph of Skip Heitzig: Fred Roybal

VP 03-06-13

"Skip turns the spotlight on the Bible, something missing in many of our Christian books today. He hits the mark when he outlines the life of Abraham and distinctly describes the Godprint that was placed upon Abraham's heart. Skip's biblical perspective shows that while Christians battle the flesh throughout life, we can learn by looking back on past mistakes that help us grow deeper in Christ. This book will leave an imprint on your life."
– Franklin Graham, President and CEO
Samaritan's Purse,
Billy Graham Evangelistic Association

"Dr. Skip Heitzig's writing style conveys the vertical voice your heart hears from above. The truth he shares is from God. There is no question in my mind that you will be impacted as you journey with Abraham, the mystic—a normal human being who left a legacy. You are left with the hope that you too can follow in his footsteps. Skip brilliantly paints pictures with words that inspire and motivate you to go beyond logic and reason to faith in the God of Abraham. This book is an overflow of Skip's personal walk with God."
– K.P. Yohannon, Gospel for Asia

"In my own personal journey with Jesus, there have been a handful of people who've made a unique mark on me. The means by which they communicate God's heart, their style of explaining His Word, and the way they're able to connect with where I'm at … it's as if they're giving me the answers to my questions before I even ask them. Without question, Pastor Skip is one of those people. His ability to break down the deep truths of God with skill and savvy is second to none, and Godprint is his latest gift to those who are passionate to not only know God, but to have their lives used by Him."
– Bob Coy, Senior Pastor
Calvary Chapel, Fort Lauderdale

Acknowledgments

Special thanks to:

Steve Halliday, Editor.

Publishing Team:
Brian Nixon, Rebekah Hanson,
and the folks at Bridge-Logos.

Contents

Blessing the Future

Carbon footprint. Have you heard that term? According to *carbonfootprint.com*, a carbon footprint is the ecological impression each person makes upon the natural world and our planet, for good or for ill. In their words, a carbon footprint is "a measure of the impact our activities have on the environment, and in particular, climate change."

In the last few years, the term has become quite popular. A quick search on Google produces hundreds of sites that offer suggestions on how to reduce one's carbon footprint.

The concept raises an interesting question for Christians: Are we supposed to leave some kind of mark? Should we care about the impression we leave? Should we be concerned with our spiritual footprint? Our legacy? Our memorial? Our heritage?

Hey, isn't it all going to burn in the end?

To fully answer this question frankly lies beyond the scope of this book. While I firmly believe we should be good stewards of God's good creation, I think we should have a far greater interest in something more than reducing our carbon footprint.

This something is what I call a "Godprint."

A Christian leaves a Godprint whenever he or she, by the power of the Holy Spirit, positively influences the world for the cause of Christ. Every Christian has the opportunity to leave a lasting, God-centered, positive impression upon the Earth.

The Bible is chockfull of people who did just this: Moses, David, Mary, Paul, and, of course, the Lord Jesus himself. However, when we want to zero in on a character who doesn't seem so different from us, and yet who left behind an enormous Godprint—a lasting legacy that continues to bless the world today—we have to mention Abraham.

The life of Abraham overflowed with adventure, crisis, fear, faith, and most importantly, God. Three major world religions point to him as a major and even foundational influence— Judaism, Christianity, and Islam. The Apostle Paul called Abraham the *"father of those who have faith"* (Romans 4:11, NLT). Yet these Godprints, as tremendous as they might be, pale in comparison to what I consider Abraham's greatest legacy: God used Abraham; Abraham didn't use God. God's fingerprints left a deep impression upon Abraham's life, and in turn, Abraham left a lasting impression upon his world.

A Godprint.

I invite you to join me as we travel back in time to learn how we can leave our own Godprints behind us on this Earth. God calls us to leave a lasting impression upon the world—and by mining certain core elements from the rich veins of Abraham's life story, we can discover how to create our own Godprints.

To bless God and to bless everyone around us—even those future generations who as yet have left no footprints at all, carbon or otherwise—this is the opportunity and the challenge that lies before us.

In His strong love,
Pastor Skip

CHAPTER ONE

Your Past:
Guidepost or Hitching Post?

I love the Italian custom of celebrating the arrival of each new year. Around midnight on New Year's Eve, the streets empty, cars disappear, pedestrians vanish, and even the police take cover. Because at twelve sharp, house windows fly open and family members toss out, right on the street, some object that reminds them of something from the past year they want to forget. It could be a vase; it could be an ornament; it could even be a piece of furniture. Does that sound radical to you?

I think it sounds like a lot of fun.

The truth is, no matter how flawed your past, your future is spotless. While your past may have done much to shape you, you don't have to let it misshape you. In fact, you can start right now to leave an imprint for good upon your world, wherever you are. Few of us feel content merely to make a buck or forge a career. We want to make a difference in the lives of those around us. We want to know that our lives count for something.

Do you want to make a mark on your world? I think God put such a desire within every human heart. By the time our lives end, we want to know that we did the right thing, we lived with good goals in mind, we lived with purpose, and we fulfilled what God called us to do.

1

Psychologist William Marsten asked three thousand people, "What do you have to live for?" It shocked him to find that 94 percent of his respondents said they were simply enduring the present while waiting for something better to happen in the future—for children to grow up and leave home, for the next year to come around, for another chance to take a long-anticipated vacation.

What would you say if Marsten asked you his question? What do you have to live for?

Satan wants to get you so focused on your past that you neglect both your present and your future; it's one of his most successful ploys. Your past and all that it means has great value as a guidepost—but if you park there, it can become a hitching post, both dangerous and deadly.

Perfection Not Required

To make your mark on this world, you don't have to be perfect. You don't have to come from a prominent family, have powerful friends, or own a chain of banks. One man described in the Old Testament began with none of those things, and yet his life continues to exert a major impact on the world today.

Abram, later called Abraham, made such a mark on history that today three major world religions—Judaism, Islam, and Christianity—revere him as their patriarch or leader. All three honor Abraham as a man who left his distinctive mark on the world around him.

Or consider another indicator of this man's unusual importance: the amount of space devoted to him in the Bible. The first eleven chapters of Genesis cover roughly the two thousand years that preceded Abraham, about nineteen generations. Yet the entire middle section of Genesis—fourteen chapters—focuses on the life of this remarkable man. The New Testament further highlights the impact of Abraham. In one chapter of Romans and two chapters of Galatians, he's called "the father of all who believe." Abraham provides the model for anyone who wants to be justified by faith, not works. Hebrews 11, the Faith Hall of Fame, also shines the spotlight on him. And three times the Bible refers to Abraham as "the friend of God" (see 2 Chronicles 20:7; Isaiah 41:8; James 2:23).

How would you like God to give you such a title?

"Do you see Sharon over there? She's the friend of God."

To this day, Arabs still refer to Abraham as *el kahlil*, friend of God.

How did Abraham come to leave such a mark on the world? It certainly wasn't because of his past. Five experiences in his early life, four of which he had no control over, all shaped his past—but he did not allow them to misshape his present or future.

Experience One: Disbelief

Abraham most emphatically did not start out as a great man of faith. Does that fact surprise or even shock you? In fact, his pagan roots landed him squarely in the land of polytheism, not the land of promise.

In his day, Ur of the Chaldeans proudly functioned as the cultural center of southern Mesopotamia (present-day Iraq). The archaeologist's spade has discovered that this ancient city was not some Podunk town in the middle of the desert, but a thriving metropolis with a population of at least three hundred thousand. As the capital of Sumer, it boasted an advanced civilization. Archaeological digs have discovered musical instruments of all kinds, as well as crafts and art that speak of a sophisticated and artistic culture. The town had a library and a university that specialized in math and astronomy.

You didn't have to look far to see its pagan foundation, however. In the center of town stood an impressive temple—a ziggurat (or large tower) that spiraled up to the heavens. There the city residents worshiped several gods, including their principal god, Sin, the moon god.

(Interesting, isn't it? They didn't know it, but way back then they were worshiping sin.)

We know that Abraham's father, Terah, worshiped idols. Centuries later Joshua told his countrymen, *"... your ancestors, including Terah, the father of Abraham and Nahor, lived beyond the Euphrates River, and they worshiped other gods"* (Joshua 24:2, NLT). The ancestors of Abraham also worshiped idols. Do you suppose any of that rubbed off on Abraham? We don't know how much it may have done so, but without question he grew up in a pagan culture.

An ancient Jewish commentary known as the Midrash says that Terah crafted little idols assisted by Abram, his son. The Great Flood had already engulfed the world; the Tower of Babel had already fallen. By this time God had revealed himself powerfully in many unforgettable ways, and yet it didn't take long for corruption and decline and idolatry to regain a foothold in the ancient world, especially in Ur.

We get an idea of the depth of Ur's paganism by recalling that Abraham's grandson, Jacob, fled to Mesopotamia after he had swindled his elder brother of both his birthright and his blessing. There he married two sisters, Rachel and Leah, and after some time decided to return to Canaan. The Bible says Rachel took some household gods from her father's house (see Genesis 31:34). She stuck these little statues in the saddle of her camel. So not only did Abram's family worship idols during his boyhood years, but three generations later, his relatives in Mesopotamia still owned and venerated these idols.

Abram's early life has a lot in common with many of us. We, too, have grown up in an advanced, spiritual culture. *The New York Times* religion editor said recently that we are witnessing a mass movement of individual seekers finding spirituality, but not necessarily truth.

That's why I think we have a lot to learn from Abraham. Like most of us, he grew up in a culture of disbelief in the one true God.

Experience Two: Death

Tragedy pushed its way into the early life of Abram. His brother Haran died *"before his father"* (Genesis 11:28). One Jewish fable says that Terah's sons refused to worship the fire god, so Terah cast Haran into the furnace and let him burn to a crisp. I doubt the story's truth. In fact, to say Haran died "before" his father could simply mean that he died some time before his father did, not that he died in front of him. Whatever the case, Abram knew all about tragedy.

This man didn't skate through life unscathed from pain or sorrow or heartache. The deaths of his brother and later, his father, shaped his experience. Pain and heartache informed much of his early life.

As a pastor, I know that death can affect a family like few other experiences can. A dark cloud settles over the family for a long time. Survivors never forget the scene if they witness a loved one die in their presence; and the death notification stays forever lodged in their memory banks.

Perhaps you have had to tell someone, "Your daughter has died," or "Your son has passed away," or "Your father (or mother) is gone." The person hearing the announcement never forgets that moment so long as he or she lives.

I will never forget the night my father called to say that my brother had died. I was twenty-two years old. I can still picture the room; still feel my chaotic emotions. When those old feelings resurface, such as at funerals or when others find themselves in a similar position, I find I can get in touch with their sorrow because I never have forgotten that dark night.

Have you ever received a call like that? If so, it probably shook you up. It might even have shaken your faith to the core. Up to that point, perhaps, life seemed great and you had God all figured out. You thought you saw Him clearly—and then death stormed into your life and broke down the doors. Afterward, you didn't feel quite so sure. Maybe you even said some things in doubt or disbelief or anger at God. Maybe you felt like the bereaved Martha, who told Jesus accusingly, *"If You had been here, my brother would not have died"* (John 11:21).

Death has a way of unearthing our real view of God. It can sternly challenge our faith. And even special people—individuals like Abram, who had an extraordinary place and role picked out for him by God to make his mark on society—suffered like this. Death certainly shaped their past ... but it didn't have to misshape their present or future.

Experience Three: Disappointment

Abram also endured a great disappointment in his marriage. And, no, he didn't feel disappointed with his wife; something else in their union caused his distress. Or I should say, something else not in their union caused his distress.

Abram and Sarai had no children. Infertility plagued this couple.

Ancient cultures considered it catastrophic for a woman to fail to conceive a child. Her infertility devastated her and badly reflected on her worth as a woman and her place in the culture. And her husband—in this case, Abram—suffered deeply as well.

Pagan cultures looked at childlessness as a curse of the gods. "The moon god, the sun god, the fire god—they have cursed our marriage!" This superstition found its way even into Israel, where an ancient Hebrew wife who couldn't conceive thought God had blighted her life: "The LORD God—He has cursed our marriage!"

Many years later, Jacob, Abram's grandson, married two women. When his first wife, Leah, became pregnant, she said, *"The LORD has surely looked on my affliction"* (Genesis 29:32). An "affliction"—that's what they called infertility back then. When Rachel, Jacob's second wife (and Leah's younger sister), saw that her sister had twice given birth, she grabbed Jacob and said to him, *"Give me children, or else I die!"* (Genesis 30:1). That's a lot to put on a guy, but she did it without flinching. Rabbis eventually listed seven kinds of people as excluded from the presence of God: first, a Jew who had no wife; and second, a Jew who had a wife, but no child.

What a heavy burden to bear.

Of course, we know that later in Abram's story God miraculously intervened and gave Abram and Sarai a son in their old age. God used her infertility simply as a setup for a great miracle named Isaac. But in the meantime, neither Abram nor Sarai knew anything about what was coming.

Sarai probably grew up playing with dolls, imagining what it would be like to become a wife, have a home, cook, and cuddle her own children. When she got engaged to Abram, they no doubt asked each other, "How many kids do you want to have?" Her infertility must have especially troubled Abram, because his name means "exalted father." He had to be the laughingstock of every village he visited.

"What's your name?" they'd ask.

"Exalted father," Abram would reply.

"How many kids do you have?"

"None."

And then the laughter, scorn, and derision erupted.

Perhaps you know this feeling well. Maybe infertility comprises a part of your past or even your present. You've seen doctors; you have had people pray for you; you have been anointed with oil (you would take a bath in oil if you thought it would work). Every time a baby dedication or a Mother's Day rolls around, you feel a wave of sadness come over you. It's tough for you to hang around people celebrating their happy kids. Your infertility has frustrated your hopes, broken your heart, and deflated your spirit. Did you know that infertility affects 6.1 million women in the United States, 10 percent of the reproductive population? Sixteen out of a hundred couples struggle with infertility.

But maybe infertility isn't your problem. Perhaps the very idea of marriage brings you great disappointment. Maybe you've waited for a husband or a wife. You fully expected to be married by now—but you're not.

Or maybe you expected to be healed from a disease by now—and you're not.

Perhaps you thought you'd get that raise at work—but they didn't give it to you. In fact, they even lowered your wage.

Maybe you thought, "The court will surely rule in my favor"—but it hasn't turned out that way.

Pain and disappointment help to form who we are. We bring our disappointments with us, into this very moment. These hurts are very real, just as they were in Abram's time.

Some people, unfortunately, choose to park their lives in that place of disappointment. Their past becomes a hitching post rather than a guidepost. They repeatedly go back to their past and relive it and rehash it and refuse to let it go.

But nobody—including you—can grow until we finally let go of our disappointments.

Experience Four: Displacement

Abram also had to deal with the effects of displacement. One day his father, Terah, took his whole family to a city named Haran, and there the family lived for many years. If it wasn't bad enough to have to endure disbelief, a death, and the disappointment of infertility, now Abram had to suffer through the displacement of everything he knew growing up. Gone were the familiar hometown, his friends, and most of his relatives. Dad simply got up and moved the whole family with him.

Several years ago Dr. Thomas Holmes did a well-known study on stress. He identified several major stress factors—the death of a loved one, changing jobs, moving away, getting married, etc.—and assigned a certain value to each one. He figured that if a person accumulated two to three hundred of these stress points within a year or so, that person would wind up in tough shape.

So what happens when we apply Dr. Holmes's findings to Abram? Holmes assigned sixty-three stress factor points to the death of a close family member; Abram suffered two deaths in the period of a few years. Holmes assigned fifty-three points to a major personal injury or illness. Marriage counted for fifty points. A change in the health of a family member brought forty-four points, while a change in residence amounted to twenty points.

If I have counted correctly, Abram had amassed more than three hundred stress points.

Abram did not get a "free pass" through the early part of his life. And then consider this: as he grew up, he had no real spiritual resources to cope with any of this.

Experience Five: Disobedience

The first four experiences I have highlighted from Abram's early years lay largely out of his control. Who can control the death of a brother, or the infertility of a wife, or the religious values passed down from parents to children? How could Abram prevent his father from saying one fine morning, "Okay, folks, pack it up. We're all moving to Haran"? Abram didn't have much say over any of those things.

But disobedience? That one he could control.

When Terah decided to move his family, he chose a city of the same name as his deceased son. He made his way westward along the Euphrates River and stopped at Haran. Why stop there?

Apparently Terah had decided to return home. A close look at his genealogical records reveals that many names in his family tree bear the same name as this town. Most historians therefore believe Terah traced his roots back to Haran; probably he was born there. And some unknown period of time after his birth, a large number of people emigrated from Haran and traveled six hundred miles east to Ur of the Chaldees.

In moving to Haran, however, Terah stood directly in the path of a divine command given to Abram: *"Now the LORD had said* [not said at this point, but earlier had said] *to Abram, 'Get out of your country* [he did that], *from your family* [he didn't do that], *and from your father's house* [he didn't do that], *to a land that I will show you* [he didn't do that]'"* (Genesis 12:1). Terah wanted to skip the large basin of desert between Haran and Canaan, where God had told Abram to go.

Maybe Abram had told his dad—still shaken up over his son's death—about the divine instructions he had received. Or maybe a heartbroken Terah simply wanted to go home. Whatever the truth, Terah decided to take his remaining family back to where he had grown up. And so Abram stayed in Haran until his father died, even though God had called him to move on to Canaan. Interestingly, the name Terah means "delay," and this dad, bless his heart, delayed his son from obeying God's calling for at least five, and maybe as many as fifteen, years.

In fact, Abram didn't obey the Lord until verse 4: *"So Abram departed as the LORD had spoken to him, and Lot went with him. And Abram was seventy-five years old when he departed from Haran."*

Could we be misreading this text and therefore misjudging Abram for something he didn't really do? Not likely. Many centuries later a godly young man named Stephen recounted this episode from Abram's life for the Jewish religious leaders in Jerusalem. And he made clear Abram's failure to fully obey God's instructions:

> *The God of glory appeared to our father Abraham when he was in Mesopotamia, before he dwelt in Haran, and said to him, "Get out of your country and from your relatives and come to a land that I will show you."* Then he came out of the land of the Chaldeans and dwelt in Haran. And from there, when his father was dead, *He moved him to this land in which you now dwell.* (Acts 7:2-4, emphasis mine)

There's no doubt about it: God had given Abram his marching orders before Terah ever moved his family to Haran. Perhaps God had appeared to Abram in some glorious vision and said to him in Ur of the Chaldees, "Leave this place and your extended family. I want you to get a new start in a new land."

And Abram didn't do it.

Abram had enough faith to start out, but his faith soon faltered. It was still weak. He was just learning the ropes of faith. At this time Abram was not yet a mature believer; in fact, he was barely a believer at all. He had enough faith to believe God and so leave Ur, but he got only halfway to Canaan before he stopped. In other words, Abram did one of the things God had commanded (leave Ur), but he neglected to fulfill the rest (leave his father and extended family and move to Canaan).

I'm not denying that Abram had it tough. He had almost no spiritual resources. The death of his brother had shaped him. Hardship had shaped him. The infertility of his wife had shaped him. And so he stayed for a long time where God didn't want him to stay. As a fledgling believer, he didn't obey fully.

And yet despite all of that, he didn't let his past become a weight that kept him from going (eventually) where God wanted him to go.

Don't let your past become a weight. You can hold on to something so dearly that it becomes a burden instead of a balloon, a hitching post instead of a guidepost. Whatever you bring with you from your old life into your new life in Christ can create problems. They did for Abram, and they will for you, too.

Two Life Lessons

Abram's early life teaches us two primary lessons about making a positive mark in this life.

The past has shaped you, but you don't have to let it stifle you.

All of us have a wagonload of baggage that has helped to shape who we are. Where we grew up, who raised us, what values were given to us, the trauma and pain, delights and joys—all sorts of life experiences go into the baggage that we carry into our Christian life. You and I need to learn to face these things without letting them stop us from fulfilling God's plan or will for our lives.

I have met too many people who hide behind the past: "I am this way because when I was young _____ [fill in the blank]." Or, "I am this way because I'm Irish [or German, or Latino, or African-American, or Indo-European-Micronesian-Inuit Eskimo, or whatever]." We must learn to use our past as a springboard, not as a sofa. Let's make it a teacher, not an undertaker.

Remember what Paul said? To paraphrase, "All that was past for me I have learned to count as loss and I look ahead for the prize. Forgetting the things which are behind, I look forward to the things which are ahead." (See Philippians 3:13.)

Your failures? Let them go! Your hurts? Let them go! Remember that even the heroes of the faith, revered men such as Abram, had their own baggage. They hurt and had deep disappointments and had less than ideal religious upbringings—and sometimes they started out in failure. But they kept going.

The first time you tried to walk, you fell. Even though your parents looked at you and considered you Olympic material for sure, you fell.

The first time you tried to swim, you almost drowned.

The first time you tried to hit a ball, you connected with nothing but air.

The first time you got a report card, you didn't get straight A's—and if you did, nobody in the whole school liked you.

That's life. We're not perfect. We don't start out where we need to go. We have to learn some important things along the way. For that reason, it's wonderful to read that Abram didn't start out being perfect. He stumbled as he came out of the gates. This man, biblical Abram, had a lot in common with a much later, nineteenth-century Abraham.

This subsequent Abraham failed in his first business, lost a lot of money, and quit. The next year he ran for public

13

office and lost. Two years later he tried again and won this time, but his girlfriend died the following year. The next year he had a nervous breakdown. Two years later he lost another electoral race, followed by another political defeat two years after that, followed by yet another defeat three years later. He won an election three years after that, but lost again in another two years. He tried for a higher office two years later, but lost. He waited six more years to try for the second highest office in the country, and lost. He set his sights a little lower the next time, and lost again.

That's a lot of failure. That's a lot of defeats. And yet this man, Abraham Lincoln, eventually won election to the presidency of the United States of America. And year after year, polls name him as either the best or second-best president in the history of our nation.

In much the same way, Abram, the patriarch, had a past that included failure.

Death.

Disappointment.

Displacement.

Disobedience.

While all of these things marked him, nevertheless he went on to make his own mark. His past certainly shaped him, but he didn't allow it to stifle him.

And if we want to make our mark on the world, we have to learn to follow his example.

Disobedience postpones influence.

Abram eventually made a huge mark on the world. But he could have gotten a head start on his remarkable legacy had he not delayed those five to fifteen years in Haran. He wasted a great deal of valuable time—and his disobedience postponed his influence.

Benjamin Franklin said, "For the want of a nail, the shoe is lost. For the loss of a shoe, the horse is lost. For the loss of a horse, the rider is lost. For the loss of the rider, the battle is lost. For the loss of the battle, the war is lost. And for the loss of the war, the nation is lost."

I would add, "For the want of obedience, your influence is lost."

Don't let that happen to you. Sometime this week, mull over a few of the monumental things in your past that have shaped who you are. Face them; deal with them. Realize, "That's who I am."

But don't stop there! Keep in mind who you are, but also set some priorities for your future. You can't return to the past or turn back the clock, but God can wind it up again. Right now, beginning right where you are—no matter your age or background—you can make a mark on your culture.

Don't let any of the circumstances of your past keep you from moving forward. Trust God. Lean on Him. Depend on Him. He's the Lord! And as that same Lord worked in the life of Abram, so He wants to work in your life. So move ahead. Go for it!

> *There was a very cautious man who never laughed or played,*
> *He never risked, he never tried, he never sang or prayed.*
> *And when he one day passed away, his insurance was denied;*
> *For since he never really lived, they claimed he never died.*

I don't want to die that way. Do you? I want to die going for it, moving ahead in faith by the power and will of God. That's the only way for you and me to make an indelible mark on our world.

MEDITATING ON THE MARK

In this chapter we learned that Christians must first "get over the past and look to the future" before they can truly make their mark for Christ. In our Christian walk, we must understand there is a past, present, and future.

Past. One of Satan's ploys tries to turn the focus from your present and your future to your past. On what in your past do you most tend to focus? How can you prevent this from warping your future and wasting your time?

Present. Evaluate your personal walk with Christ at this very moment. How close is your fellowship? How regularly do you attend church? List some ways in which you can strengthen your personal Christian walk today.

Future. God put within us a desire to do the right thing. What do you have to live for? On whom or what would you like to make your mark? List some practical ways in which you can begin to do so.

MODELING THE MASTER'S MARK

Past. Philippians 3:13-14: *"Forgetting those things which are behind and reaching forward to those things which are ahead, I press toward the goal for the prize of the upward call of God in Christ Jesus."*

Present. Colossians 3:16-17: *"Let the word of Christ dwell in you richly in all wisdom, teaching and admonishing one another in psalms and hymns and spiritual songs, singing with grace in your hearts to the Lord. And whatever you do in word or deed, do all in the name of the Lord Jesus, giving thanks to God the Father through Him."*

Future. Jeremiah 29:11: *"For I know the thoughts that I think toward you, says the* LORD, *thoughts of peace and not of evil, to give you a future and a hope."*

MAKING YOUR MARK

Purpose today to read the Bible and apply its message in a concrete fashion. Read Psalm 1. Write out verses 1-3. Memorize verse 3.

CHAPTER TWO

Buckle Up!
You're Going on an Adventure

In an airport on my way home to Arizona, I once saw an interesting component of an airline's advertising campaign: "Feel free to actually enjoy what you do," it instructed passersby.

I smiled and said, "Well, thank you. I actually do enjoy what I do."

A short while later I spotted a second poster from the same airline that intrigued me even more. A big banner on a wall read, "Buckle up, you're going on an adventure."

Nice sentiment—but really? The company was selling rides from one city to another, nothing more. And they call that an adventure? Not if you spend too many hours in airports.

The ad did get me thinking about real adventure. I am convinced the Christian life offers the greatest adventure in the world. Excitement, danger, reward, risk, companionship, solitude, laughter, tears—it has it all. And it promises staggering rewards to boot.

As I look at the lives of many Christians, however, "adventure" seems conspicuously missing. Even though the will of God revealed and followed does, indeed, yield the greatest adventure of all, too many of us fail to get excited about asking the Lord, "What's next, God? What do You have in store?"

Peggy Noonan, a speechwriter for former president Ronald Regan, said something that continues to stick with me: "It is odd that some Christians see themselves just as the media does, as bland guys in gray suits with gray buzz cuts," she wrote. "They ought to see themselves as a young Marlon Brando on a Harley, for they are the true anti-establishment, the true rebels with a cause."

My heart leaped at her words. *Yeah!* I thought. *Get me on that Harley!* The Christian life ought to be the most exciting thing in the world.

Is it for you?

Think of it this way: Your destination is already set. You're going to Heaven—so why not enjoy the ride? Why not delight in the scenery? Why not make an adventure out of it? I don't mean you won't have to suffer. I don't mean you can escape trials or heartache or hardship. On this winding road you'll find hairpin turns, bumps, and potholes. I think it would be boring otherwise, but the scenery is truly outstanding. Nothing compares to a vital Christian experience. It's an adventure with a capital A.

Some time ago the Associated Press put out a news article about a fifty-two-year-old man found sleepwalking on the streets of Pasadena, California. It's dangerous enough to live in Pasadena, but to sleepwalk there invites catastrophe. Police found the guy walking around in a deep sleep, clad only in his pajamas, and carrying an alarm clock set to go off at 6 A.M. The officers woke him up before his alarm clock had a chance to.

That's how a lot of people live—they sleepwalk through their days. Even Christians. They don't know where they're going. They have no sense of purpose. They shuffle around in a spiritual daze, hoping that something might someday jar them out of slumber.

But people who make their mark on the world don't shuffle around aimlessly. They don't sleepwalk. People who make their mark respond appropriately to God.

Abram understood and lived out this crucial principle. This man followed God's plan for his life and discovered it to be the most exciting adventure possible. As he took one step in front of the other, his grand adventure unfolded in three profound movements:

Movement One:
The Word of God Leads to Faith in God

As this part of our story begins, Abram is seventy-five years young. Right away, that should tell you something. Age is never an obstacle to having an adventure. Somebody once said, "If wrinkles must be written upon our brows, let them not be written on our hearts." Three quarters of his way to the century mark, Abram set out on the adventure of a lifetime.

And that adventure began with a Voice. The Bible says simply, *"The LORD had said to Abram ..."* (Genesis 12:1a). That's significant, because God hadn't said anything to humankind for a very, very long time. No one had heard this Voice since the time of Noah; then followed centuries of eerie silence. But now at last God spoke once again, this time to an obscure Semite living in Ur of the Chaldees. And the Voice told Abram to leave.

"Get out of your country," [the Voice said] *"from your family, from your father's house to a land that I will show you,"* (Genesis 12:1b). Notice what God did not say. He didn't say, "Hi! My name's God. Hey, good buddy, I know who you are. Let's grab some coffee and get to know one another a little better." Far from it. Right out of the chute, God spoke to Abram in an imperative: "Leave. Get out."

That's quite an introduction!

God told Abram to leave his country, his family, and his father's house. Why? Because Abram had to make a clean break with the past in order to enter the exciting future God had planned for him. His old relationships and former ties and familiar environment could all derail his spiritual growth. So God said to him, "Get out of there."

It's no different with us. When we come to Christ in faith, we're told to repent, to turn away from the past and from those old things that once kept us tightly in their grip. "Make a clean break," God says to us. Jesus declared, *"If anyone desires to come after Me, let him deny himself, and take up his cross daily, and follow Me"* (Luke 9:23). To the extent that we leave the old life is the extent to which we will enjoy the new life.

Of course, God didn't leave it at that. Abram needed a good reason to listen to the Voice. So God said, "I'm going to bless you." And just look at His promises! First, He told Abram He would show him a new land. Second, He said:

> *I will make you a great nation; I will bless you and make your name great; and you shall be a blessing. I will bless those who bless you,... I will curse him who curses you....* (Genesis 12:2-3)

Five times in that passage I count the promise, "I will"—the five "I wills" of God. Why did He make it so emphatic? God wanted to make it crystal clear that it was Him who would be doing this: "Abram, you're going to cooperate with me because I'm calling you to obey. But let me spell it out for you right now: This is wholly of Me. This is something I'm going to do by My own might and by My own power."

Joseph Parker, a London preacher who ministered at the same time as Charles Spurgeon, said, "Great lives are trained by great promises." God promised what He'd do for Abram, what He'd do in him, and what He'd do through him.

What would God do for him? "I'll make you a great nation."

What would God do in him? "I'll bless you."

What would God do through him? "In you all the nations of the Earth shall be blessed."

People sometimes teach that the Christian life is all about what you should do for God. "Shame on you; you need to be busier for God!" But that's not where making your mark begins. Not at all.

During his inaugural address in 1961, John Kennedy became famous for telling his nation, "Ask not what your country can do for you, but ask what you can do for your country." I'll never forget his words, even though I was just a little boy at the time.

Many people today think that's how it is with God. "Ask not what God can do for you, but what you can do for God." Not so! Here's the truth: you can't do anything for God until you first realize what God promises to do for you. He promises; then we respond. The Apostle John says that we love Him because He first loved us. (See 1 John 4:19.)

God promised that He would make Abram into a great nation—and I can't help but think God broke into a big smile when He said it. Yes, it was a serious promise, but God has to have quite a sense of humor to say He intended to make a great nation out of an old guy with an infertile wife. At age seventy-five, Abram didn't have a single child … and yet God still promised him, "I'm going to make you into a great nation."

Millennia later we know what happened. Both Jews and Arabs trace their lineage back to Abram. Millions of men and women living today on planet Earth trace their family roots back to Father Abram. I find that remarkable, because studies show that despite the seventy-year Babylonian captivity in 586 BC, which thinned out the ranks of the Jews, by the first century AD, one out of every ten individuals in the Roman Empire was Jewish, tracing their lineage back to Abram.

"So what?" someone says. "I mean, what does that have to do with me? Chances are, I'm not going to become a nation."

Well, what is a nation? A nation is essentially one person's life expanded to ultimate proportions. The late biblical expositor Ray Stedman said that every nation in the Bible begins with a man. Then comes a family, and as the family grows and expands, a nation finally emerges. Every nation is nothing but the continued expanded life of a single man. In other words, God was telling Abram, "Your influence is going to be monumental."

And so it was. Abram had Isaac, and Isaac had Jacob, and Jacob had twelve sons, each of whom fathered a whole tribe. The Hebrew nation grew out of that family, eventually giving birth to kings and prophets ... and ultimately to Jesus. That has to be the primary meaning here: "... *in you all the nations of the earth will be blessed*" (Galatians 3:8). God means more than the simple fact that the nation of Israel would produce cool stuff. No, the idea was that all the nations of the Earth would be blessed because the Messiah would come through Abram.

And what does that have to do with you? Just this: God wants not only to bless you—and He has and He does and He will—but God wants to make you into a blessing. He wants to turn you into a person who will make his or her mark on this Earth, for good.

And how do you begin that process? You listen carefully to the promises and the commands of God. As Abram listened to all these promises streaming from God's mouth, something happened within him that stirred him to act. As his ears heard God's Word, faith blossomed in his heart. His example illustrates one of the most important principles in Scripture: God's Word leads to faith. The principle finds ultimate expression in Romans 10: *"So then faith comes by hearing, and hearing by the word of God"* (verse 17). As God spoke His Word and Abram listened to it and believed it, faith welled up inside him. And out of that faith, Abram responded. According to Hebrews 11, Abram's exposure to God's Word led to faith in God's promises.

This principle has not changed even a little in the last three thousand years. It still holds true today. If you want your faith to grow, then you must regularly expose yourself to God's truth. You must saturate both your heart and your mind in it. Drench yourself in God's promises as declared in the Word of God. Peter put it this way: *"As newborn babes, desire the pure milk of the word, that you may grow thereby"* (1 Peter 2:2). Get off the spiritual junk food and get into something that can really nourish you: the Word of God.

USA Today conducts a lot of small polls that appear in a corner of the front page. One recent poll reported that one in five Americans say they have never read the Bible, even though 90 percent say they own at least one copy. Boy, is that revealing!

"Yup, I own a Bible. Look at it—there it is on my table, pressing flowers. And if you open it, I can show you the names of a few of my recent ancestors."

Eighty percent of Americans call the Bible the most influential book in human history, but only 17 percent read it daily. Now, if God's Word is spiritual milk that helps you to grow, then what are 83 percent of Americans eating every day for spiritual sustenance? Junk food.

What do you eat? Remember, you are what you eat, spiritually. The Bible is written for life transformation; it will change you. As you spend time in it, your faith will grow. Martin Luther used to say, "The Bible is alive. It speaks to me. It has hands and feet. It runs after me and lays hold of me."

Movement Two:
Faith Leads to Obedience

Abram's faith led to something else. The Bible says, *"So Abram departed as the LORD had spoken to him"* (Genesis 12:4). That's obedience. Abram did what God commanded.

And did he know where he was going? No. He had no clue until he arrived. God told Abram that he was to leave Ur for "a land that I will show you." The writer of Hebrews says it like this:

> *By faith Abraham obeyed when he was called to go out to the place which he would receive as an inheritance. And he went out, not knowing where he was going.* (Hebrews 11:8)

Now, picture Abram out there in front of his tent. The moving camels/vans come up, workers put all of his furniture and possessions on them, and then the driver says, "Okay, where to?" Imagine how goofy it would sound to reply, "Well, I don't know yet, but God will show me." But that's precisely what it was like. Abram didn't know where he was going. He left his home by faith. He had no revealed destination, no GPS, no road map; just, "Go, and I'll guide you." And he went.

Faith leads to obedience.

I found an interesting quote by a seventeenth-century Puritan preacher who said all of mankind can be divided into three classes:

Class Number 1: the Intenders
Class Number 2: the Endeavorers
Class Number 3: the Performers

Terah, Abraham's father, was an Intender. He may have intended to go to Canaan, but he stopped in Haran. That's where he died. He never made it to the Promised Land.

Abram's nephew, Lot, was an Endeavorer; he got to the Promised Land, but he constantly failed to walk by faith.

Abram and Sarai, on the other hand, were Performers. They listened, they believed, and then they acted. And that's the way it has to be if you want to make a significant mark on your world.

Hearing must always lead to heeding. If you're always hearing truth but never doing the truth, you will become a calloused, dangerous individual. No wonder James admonishes us with such tough words:

> *Brothers and sisters, what's the use of saying you have faith if you don't prove it by your actions ... Faith that doesn't show itself by good deeds is no faith at all—it is dead and useless.* (James 2:14, 17, NLT).

Do you know that the Bible contains 7,146 promises? God made more than 7,000 promises of what He would do for us. Now, there's your ticket to adventure!

So what do you do with the promises of God? "I underline them," you say. Fine, but that's not the best answer.

"I memorize them." Good, but not the best.

You should say, "I live by them. I bank on them. I stand on them. I trust them implicitly and totally." That's the right answer! If it's really God's Word, then we must act upon it.

During the settling of our country, a man tried to cross the Mississippi River in early winter around nightfall. It had iced over. He couldn't determine the thickness of the ice and no bridge spanned the river at that location, so he decided to get down on all fours and crawl over the frozen river. He wanted to spread his weight out, lest he break the ice and fall through to the frigid waters below. Halfway across the river he heard singing behind him. He looked back and saw a man riding a horse-drawn carriage, weighed down with a heavy load. As the man drove across the ice, he sang at the top of his lungs, thoroughly enjoying himself. Imagine how the guy stretched out on all fours felt at that moment. "I feel like an idiot doing this. The ice is obviously thick enough for me to stand up." And so he did.

Remember the old hymn, "Standing on the Promises (of Christ My King)"? If we were honest, a lot of us would have to sing, "Creeping on the promises of Christ my King." Others might even have to say, "Sitting on the promises." They haven't even reached the creeping stage yet.

George Müller, a man of great faith and action who lived in Bristol, England, more than a century ago, ran an orphanage, primarily by faith. He claimed that we could overcome 90 percent of our difficulties when our hearts became ready to do the Lord's will, whatever it might be.

That's a good summary of Abram's life thus far. "I'm going to do whatever the Lord asks me to do." He heard God's Word, it produced faith in his heart, and his faith led to obedience.

Movement Three:
Obedience Leads to Blessing

Abram obeyed God, headed east, and eventually came to a place called Shechem, a town in the Promised Land near what would later be called Samaria. By then the Canaanites—the future enemies of Israel—already lived in the land. And at that point the Lord appeared to Abram and said, "To your descendants I will give this land."

Abram immediately built an altar to the Lord. Soon he moved from that place to the mountains east of Bethel (which in Hebrew means, "house of God"). There he built another altar to God and called upon the name of the Lord.

Did you notice what happened? As soon as Abram heard the command and the promises, he got up and obeyed. And as soon as he obeyed, God appeared to him and gave Abram a new sense of His presence and a new promise. It's the first time we read about God appearing to Abram.

Apparently, God did not appear to Abram the first time He made contact; He simply spoke. Abram didn't see anything. But in Genesis 12, verse 7, once Abram obeyed and went, God appeared to him. Abram saw a holy apparition: a *theophany*, an incredible, divine display, right in front of him. That seems exceedingly significant to me, for it means that the revelation of God gets clearer and greater with each step of obedience we take.

We find this principle throughout the Bible. With every step of obedience that you take toward God, God reveals more of himself to you. James says it like this: *"Draw near to God and He will draw near to you"* (James 4:8). It's as if God is waiting for your move. So move! Move in obedience and you'll find that He's there to reveal greater secrets of who He is. Obedience brings a new sense of God's presence. In a similar way, Hebrews 11 tells us that God rewards those who diligently seek Him. So Abram diligently sought God, and God rewarded Abram with a renewed sense of His presence and promise.

At this point I'd like to make a quick comparison between two primary ways of approaching life. You can choose which of the two seems best.

First, there's what we could call "the way of the world." Genesis 11 tells the memorable story of the Tower of Babel. The people there built a huge ziggurat that towered toward the heavens. They said, *"Come, let us build ourselves a city, and a tower whose top is in the heavens; let us make a name for ourselves ... "* (v. 4).

Abram's brother, Nahor, apparently had a lot in common with these folks. In Genesis 24 we read that he, Nahor, had a whole city named after himself back in Mesopotamia. Suppose you asked his neighbors, "Hey, tell me about Nahor. Ever heard of him?"

"Nahor?" they'd say. "What a success story! He's a Fortune 500 guy. He's even got his own city. Very successful."

And then suppose you asked, "Whatever happened to that Abram guy, his brother, he used to hang out with?"

"Oh, that guy. He left a long time ago to 'follow God.' That's what he said, anyway. We haven't seen him since. But Nahor—now, there's a stud!"

That's "the way of the world."

Second, there's the "way of God." Remember what God told Abram: "I will bless you and I will make your name great." Do you see the contrast? The folks back in Babel said, "We're going to make a name for ourselves." Abram said, "Forget that. I'm going to follow God. He told me to go." And God said, "And I'll make your name great."

It's your choice. You can try to make a name for yourself, like the men of Babel; or you can partner with God and allow Him to make your name great, like Abram. But before you choose, consider this: if you're going to leave your mark, make sure it's eternal. One day this life will end and you'll come face-to-face with God. Eternity will stretch out before you—and the only marks that will last are the ones that God took the lead in making.

How Do You Hear?

People who make their mark are people who respond to God, like Abram. He listened. He obeyed. And God blessed him because of it.

It all goes back to the Word of God. The catalyst for every good thing in this entire story is found in God's Word and in Abram's response to it. Abram heard and Abram obeyed.

So let me ask you: How are you hearing?

"Oh, my hearing's just fine, Skip. Thanks for asking."

No, that's not what I asked. How are you listening?

"What do you mean, how am I listening? I am reading this, aren't I?"

Sure, but there are a lot of ways to hear the same message. Jesus often said, *"He who has ears to hear, let him hear"* (Luke 8:8). I imagine people thought, "What is he talking about? Ears? I have two of them." But that's not what He meant, was it? He also said, *"Take heed how you hear"* (Luke 8:18).

Some people listen very actively. You see them get attentive every time truth gets mentioned. Every time you see a Bible lying open, they're taking notes. They're zeroed in; they never look around; they're into it.

Most people don't listen actively; they listen passively, mechanically. They don't really hear.

President Franklin Roosevelt once grew tired of all the dinner meetings he had to host at the White House. He just didn't care for the formality of it all. He doubted that many of his guests really listened to anything he had to say and he suspected they just wanted to meet the president. So one night he tried an experiment.

After his speech, all the guests formed a line to meet him. He said something to each one, to test whether they were listening. A guest would shake his hand, then he would smile back and say, "I murdered my grandmother this morning."

And no one blinked an eye. They all responded, "How lovely, Mister President," or "Keep up the good work, Mister President."

Except for one foreign diplomat.

When the president said, "I murdered my grandmother this morning," the man bent close to Roosevelt and answered, "She probably deserved it, Mister President."

G. Campbell Morgan, one of my favorite authors, said:

> I now affirm that it is impossible to read this book [the Bible] without being aware that it makes an appeal to our conscience and will. Whenever it does that, whenever it captures our conviction, the student must respond by obedience, or inevitably this becomes a sealed book.

I believe the reason why so many believers have lost their love for the Bible is they have failed to recognize the necessity for obedience to the moral claims God makes in His Word. Perhaps we ought to put a big sign on every Bible that says, "WARNING: THIS COULD BE THE MOST DANGEROUS BOOK IN THE WORLD."

If you listen to God's Word without an aim to obey it, your heart will become calloused. Eventually you'll be able to listen time and time again, but never manage a better response than, "Well, that was ... okay. On a scale of one to ten, I'd give it a four. Nice beat. Easy to dance to, but too long."

God demands obedience. If we don't listen, believe, act on our faith, and obey, we're not going to receive God's blessing. We'll be like spiritual zombies. No wonder the writer of Hebrews said, "*We must give the more earnest heed to the things we have heard, lest we drift away"* (Hebrews 2:1).

Are you drifting?

There's no good reason to drift, of course. You can utterly depend on God's promises—even the ones that seem most unlikely.

For centuries after the Romans exiled the Jews from their homeland, the nation of Israel had no land. It seemed that it would always be that way. In fact, in 1932, even G. Campbell Morgan said, "I am now convinced that the teaching of the Scripture as a whole is that there is no future for Israel as an earthly people at all." I can understand why he'd say that. It had been nearly two thousand years, and the Jews still had no homeland.

If only he'd waited a few years.

On May 14, 1948, the modern state of Israel became a reality, in fulfillment of biblical prophecy. And it still stands today. Queen Victoria once had a discussion about the Bible with her prime minister. "Show me one thing that proves the Scriptures are true," she insisted.

The prime minister smiled and said, "The Jew, Madam. The Jew."

God's promises are based on His holy character and flawless track record. He's absolutely reliable. He can handle your rent payment; He can handle your bad marriage. He can handle whatever's happening with you at work. He can handle your future, just as He promised.

The question is, will you believe His promises?

Abram teaches us that exposure to truth develops faith, faith leads to obedience, and obedience brings a divine blessing. So let's get out on the road and enjoy the adventure. Let's determine to make our mark on this world … one that will last for eternity.

MEDITATING ON THE MARK

In this chapter we learned that the Christian life is not to be the life of a sleepwalker, adrift in a spiritual daze. In fact, we are called to respond appropriately to God in three distinct movements—that faith leads to obedience, and obedience leads to blessing.

Faith. We know that the Word of God leads to faith. What are you doing with the Word of God? How often do you actively delve into Scripture?

Obedience. We cannot do anything for God until we realize what the promises in Christ do for us. How do you respond to His promises? Are you trusting in them or trivializing them? Explain.

Blessing. God is waiting for your move. As soon as you obey, He will give you a new sense of His presence and a new promise. What's your move?

MODELING THE MASTER'S MARK

Faith. Romans 10:17: *"So then faith comes by hearing, and hearing by the word of God."*

Obedience. 2 Corinthians 1:20-22: *"For all the promises of God in Him are Yes, and in Him Amen, to the glory of God through us. Now He who establishes us with you in Christ and has anointed us is God, who also has sealed us and given us the Spirit in our hearts as a guarantee."*

Blessing. James 4:8: *"Draw near to God and He will draw near to you."*

MAKING YOUR MARK

Make a list of three promises of God which you most need to rely on today. Carry these three promises with you throughout the week and commit them to memory.

CHAPTER THREE

Warning:
Doubt Can Be
Hazardous to Your Health

In 1994, an angry customer brought a lawsuit against the McDonald's corporation for serving scalding hot coffee.[1] Soon afterward, the company began affixing a big, bold warning label to all its coffee cups: "HOT."

Nearly everything today carries warning labels, mostly because of lawsuits. One of my staff members gave me a chain saw for my birthday. A warning page cautioned me, "Do not operate chain saw while upset." I thought, *These people have seen too many horror movies.*

Then I grew curious about what other things in my house might carry odd warning labels. One day I set out my favorite hot sauce on the table and read: "Warning: Must be strong to handle this sauce. Keep out of the reach of children. Do not play tricks on the weak or elderly with this sauce." No joke. It's almost as if they knew I'd buy their product.

Then I found a book called *101 Real Dumb Warning Labels.*[2] Let me give you a few examples:

One brand of hair color warns: "Warning: Do not use as an ice cream topping."

On a car sunshade you read: "Warning: Remove shade before operating vehicle."

A blow-dryer carries the advisory: "Warning: Do not use while sleeping."

A note with an iron advised: "Warning: Never iron clothes while on the body."

A label on a mattress cautioned: "Warning: Do not attempt to swallow." I'd like to see someone try that one.

Abram could probably tell you a thing or two about warning signs, or at least about warning signs that we should all take seriously. Over one sad episode in his life he would surely post: "Warning: Doubt and disbelief may be hazardous to your health."

Sea Legs

Children are quick to believe, but they also get frightened easily. They want to trust Mom and Dad, but sometimes they're fearful. I remember the day my father tried to get me to jump off a diving board into a swimming pool.

"Jump," he told me.

"No," I replied firmly.

"Go ahead, jump; you'll be okay."

"No, I'll die."

"No, you won't die; I'll catch you. Don't worry."

"No."

Finally, I jumped. The sad thing is that I was thirty years old at the time. (Not really!)

When you first start out in your life of faith, it's something like being a child, isn't it? Although the Apostle Paul rightly referred to Abraham as *the father of all those who believe* (Romans 4:11), Abraham also provided us with a classic example of what not to do. But to be fair, we have to remember that he was just starting out in his walk of faith. He was a fledgling believer. He was just getting his sea legs, you might say, when it came to trusting God.

Through this sad incident of doubt and unbelief, Abram learned a valuable lesson: it is safer to trust God when the cupboards are bare than to be out of His will in a land of abundance.

Abram failed his first test of faith in the Promised Land—but that encourages me. Do you know why? It's because the Bible never flatters its heroes. It never paints a rosy, airbrushed picture of the men and women God uses. Instead, Scripture always tells the truth about their flaws and foibles and failures. And in this case, Abram failed an early test of his faith.

Getting Used to Them

Understand that it's normal for a believer's faith to get tested. Your faith will be tested; so will mine. So how do you respond when it happens? What should you do?

A homeowner felt very proud of his perfectly green lawn. However, one summer dandelions sprouted all over his yard. He tried everything he could think of to get rid of them but nothing worked. The noxious weeds overran his property. Exasperated, he finally wrote to the Department of Agriculture. "I've tried everything," he wrote. "What should I do next?"

The return note simply said, "Try getting used to them."

When it comes to tests of faith, we could all use that advice. Get used to them. You'll have them, and so will I. But also receive a word of encouragement. As you go through a hard period of testing—even a furnace of testing—understand that God has His eye on the clock and His hand on the thermostat. He knows what you can take and will not allow the test to destroy you. You can count on that.

But don't be surprised when the road gets difficult.

God gave Abram tremendous promises, enough for him to willingly leave his comfortable home in Ur and depart for Canaan, sight unseen—but soon after he arrived, this land of promise dried up. A severe famine ensued.

When we get hungry today, we go to the grocery store and buy whatever we need. Not so in those days. Back then, famine meant life or death. The ancients lived much closer to the land than we do and had far fewer options.

Abram had come to Canaan from Ur of the Chaldeans, where the mighty Tigris and Euphrates rivers form a fertile delta that allows residents to grow crops year-round. Abram probably had never experienced a famine before he moved to Canaan. He probably quickly discovered that this new land of promise depended entirely upon its annual rainfall, a few small rivers, and very little irrigation. If the early and late rains didn't come as expected, crops failed and famine ruined the land. That's the dismal scene that greeted Abram.

Does that seem odd to you? Why would God allow a famine to ravage Canaan right after the Lord told Abram to move there? What was the point? Abram didn't know it, but God had enrolled him in a class we might call Faith 101. It was high time for Abram to go to school. God used the famine as a session to teach His young believer some lessons about faith.

Faith is like a muscle. If you want a muscle to grow stronger, you must force it to work against strong resistance. So you stack up the weights and you pump iron. It may hurt, but it's the only way your muscle will gain strength.

How would you ever know if your faith had any value unless it was tested? Anyone can talk about trusting God and believing in the Lord when the cupboards are full. It's easy to believe God when the economy is great, you have plenty of money in the bank, and life smiles at you. In those sunny days, you can talk about trusting God all day long without breaking a sweat.

But what happens when famine hits the land, when hardship comes, when trouble rumbles your way?

You may be enjoying the fat of the land right now. Life is good—never better. Great! God bless you. Enjoy it as a gift from God. But then again, your experience may be far different. Everywhere you look, life seems desolate, dry, bleak. And you wonder: *Why has this happened to me?*

It has happened because God wants you to grow stronger. None of us can grow spiritually on a steady diet of blessings. If God blessed us every day and kept all hardship away, then we'd start to see hardship as an anti-blessing. And if that happened, how would we ever know if our faith had real value?

A little story about golf balls captured my attention. When manufacturers first started producing golf balls, they thought the smoother the ball, the farther it would travel. But they soon discovered the opposite was true. The ball actually flies farther when it gets roughed up a little. So they started manufacturing golf balls with dimples all over their surfaces. Those "flaws" and "beatings" help the ball fly farther.

Why does God allow you to go through some trials? Maybe He wants you to fly a little farther.

The Bubble Pops

When the famine hit Canaan, Abram didn't look first to God. Instead, he turned his face toward Egypt. No doubt Egypt felt much more like "home" to Abram than did Canaan. After all, the Nile River basin was the breadbasket of the ancient world. His family was starving and, like anyone, he wanted to leave a place without food and go to a place of abundance. So Abram fled to Egypt (see Genesis 12:10-20).

The problem was that God never told Abram to go to Egypt. God told Abram to go to Canaan. He said, "I'm going to bless you in that land." There's absolutely no indication in the Bible that God ever told Abram to move to Egypt—the idea was all Abram's.

In Scripture, Egypt often serves as an example of the world. It has the Nile River, it regularly provides food for its people, and you don't have to live by faith there. The Bible often depicts traveling to Egypt as trusting in the resources of the world and backsliding from a life of faith. Sometimes God told His people to go to Egypt for protection or even for life, but more often than not Egypt is a kind of spiritual cop-out, a place of not trusting God and returning to the flesh. It's a place where faith takes a backseat. So we read:

> *Woe to those who go down to Egypt for help, and rely on horses, who trust in chariots because they are many, and in horsemen because they are very strong, but who do not look to the Holy One of Israel, nor seek the LORD!* (Isaiah 31:1)

But put yourself in Abram's sandals for a moment. He was a new believer who listened to God, was welled up with faith, and moved to Canaan as instructed. But almost as soon as he arrived, a famine devoured the land. I wonder if he thought, *This is the Promised Land God told me about? This is the land of blessing?*

Abram's journey of faith parallels our own. Think about it: You heard the gospel, you responded, you believed, you trusted Christ, and received Him as your Lord and Savior. If you were to describe your early life as a Christian, you probably lived in a bubble of wonder and joy. You could see everything so clearly. You thought, *Wow! Why didn't I do this earlier?*

But then one day, the bubble popped. Do you remember when it happened? Some event or circumstance came into your life that deeply challenged your spiritual walk. It tested your faith—maybe even brutally.

This uncomfortable truth often surprises some young Christians. It astonishes and stuns them because they enter the Christian faith with false notions and unrealistic expectations. Here they are, following Christ, and then something bad happens. When they pick themselves up off the floor, they indignantly ask, "*This* is the Promised Land?"

As a young Christian, I had a Honda motorcycle. I took it to an event one night where I played in the band and helped preach the gospel. I obeyed God. I gave Him my resources and my time. It was a wonderful night—but apparently somebody didn't like the message. He poured gas all over my motorcycle; it exploded and our building caught on fire. I thought: *Oh great, God! Following You gets my motorcycle blown up. Everything was working great before I received You.*

Why do hard things like this happen when we enter the "Promised Land"? When the bubble pops, when the testing comes, when the hardship arrives, you've reached a critical time. At that very point you feel tempted to go back to Egypt—to return to a familiar, more comfortable place. You might think: *It's okay to trust God, so long as everything goes okay and things go my way.* But when trouble and hardship and famine arrive, we sometimes start looking to the world for help.

Maybe you're single—for much too long, in your view. Perhaps you've come to a breaking point. You say, "Lord, look. I've given you enough time. I've trusted you. And yet I'm still single. So I guess I'll have to do this thing myself. I'll just find some nice, unsaved person, date him, and marry him."

Be very, very careful. Any step away from the Lord's will is a step toward Egypt. And that's never a step toward blessing.

On His Own

Without God's instructions to do so, Abram left the Promised Land to move to Egypt. Just before he left, he hatched a plan designed to save his skin. Abram stopped his entourage and had a little chat with his wife, Sarai. He buttered her up and said, "You know, honey, you're really beautiful."

"Why, thank you, sweetie."

"No, I mean really beautiful. In fact, you're so beautiful that when we get into this land, they might kill me to get you. So here's my strategy. We'll lie. We'll tell everyone you're my sister. Then no one will have a reason to kill me."

Now, keep in mind that this man is the *"father of all those who believe."* He's Mr. Faith. And his announced, premeditated strategy is: "Let's lie through our teeth."

To be completely accurate, Abram's lie contained a half-truth. According to Genesis 20, Sarai really was his half-sister. They had different mothers but the same father. But a half-truth is also a half-lie, and Abram proposed this story in an attempt to deceive those who might want what he had. History tells us that he had good reason to fear for his life.

Egyptians really liked Semitic women. In fact, they preferred the beauty of Semites above that of their own women. Egyptian men used to say that their own women faded too quickly. So the rulers of ancient Egypt commonly took for themselves any Semitic woman they considered beautiful. And what if the woman was married? No problem—they just killed the husband. Abram knew about this chilling custom.

If you know this story, you probably have a question at this point. "Wait a minute," you say. "Sarai is sixty-five years old—and Abram is worried?"

Isn't that cool? Sixty-five years old and she's still a knockout! (Of course, she lived to the age of one-hundred-

and-twenty-seven, so being sixty-five made her middle-aged.) Abram knew how the lusty and powerful Egyptian men would react to his gorgeous wife, and so he tried to cover his bases. He decided to lie. The problem is that one sin leads to another. Abram went from trust to doubt—and then from doubt to scheming.

At this point in Scripture, it's no accident that we see no mention of God. We hear nothing of Abram talking to God about the famine or asking for God's direction. We see no prayer, no worship. After Abram builds an altar in Canaan, we have no record of him fellowshiping with God until he returns to Canaan (see Genesis 13). He leaves all of that behind. It's gone; it's past. He's taking this Egyptian adventure all on his own.

I took four years of Spanish in school but never became very fluent. I know a few Spanish words and can pronounce them well enough so that some people think, *Oh, he speaks Spanish.* No, I don't. But I do remember one interesting linguistic characteristic. It involves the word "Lord." In Spanish, the same word that means "Mister" also means "Lord." To say *Señor Gonzalez* means "Mr. Gonzalez," but you say *El Señor Jesus* to mean "the Lord Jesus." *El Señor* means "the Lord."

We have a similar problem in English, but almost in reverse. So often we say, "Master" when we really mean "Mister." We call Jesus "Lord" but treat Him like He's just another nice guy.

That's the problem Abram had in this incident. He called God "Lord," but he didn't completely trust Him with his life. And it led to big trouble.

No Altar in Egypt

Abram had every reason to believe that the Egyptians would note his wife's beauty and want her for themselves.

And sure enough, when the couple reached Egypt, reports of Sarai's beauty quickly reached the ears of the pharaoh. In no time at all he took her into his harem. He thanked Abram for bringing his "sister" to the land by giving him sheep, oxen, donkeys, male and female servants, and camels.

How easily Abram's scheme seemed to flow. He probably thought: *I knew it! This is great; my little plan is working. I don't see any snags. In fact, maybe ... maybe this is a sign from God! Because, after all, if you're in the center of God's will, things just flow, right?*

Not so fast, Abram. Being in the center of God's will does not necessarily mean everything will go smoothly, seamlessly, and simply. And being out of God's will doesn't mean everything will be turbulent, tumultuous, and terrible. Every now and then I come across someone who tries to rationalize God's non-resistance—or the fact that He doesn't tackle them in the midst of their sin—as a sign of His approval. I will never forget the guy who told me, "I prayed about divorcing my wife. And I prayed about this affair, saying, 'God, if you don't want me to do this, just stop it.'"

How lame. God has already has revealed His will in the Word. God isn't going to rearrange the universe and have the stars spell out STOP when you go outside of His will. He's not going to shout, "Hey, you! I see you!" Yet some people take uninterrupted sin, or an ease in their sin, to mean God's hand must be upon their wicked schemes.

Abram had a seriously distorted picture when it seemed like a blessing flowed from his lie. The Bible implies that Pharaoh gave Abram all kinds of expensive gifts, apparently in exchange for Sarai's presence in the royal household. For a time, at least, Abram might have thought, *Wow! Not only is my plan going better than I could have hoped, but I'm also getting rich because of it.*

But it didn't last.

F. B. Meyer, an English commentator, wrote, "The world may treat us well, but that will be a poor compensation for our losses. There is no altar in Egypt; there is no fellowship with God; there are no promises."

If you ever feel tempted to go back and trust in the world again, think about that. Stop and ask yourself a crucial question: Is it really worth it? Is what you might gain worth what you will surely lose?

Abram discovered the answer a little too late.

Every Action

From the moment Pharaoh took Sarai under his roof, the Lord sent plagues on the king's entire household. That got his attention; the pagan king quickly learned the truth about the relationship between Sarai and Abram.

A livid Pharaoh summoned Abram into his presence, rebuked him for his lie, and then sent him away with Sarai, along with the gifts of sheep, oxen, donkeys, and servants that Abram had accepted earlier. Abram departed from Egypt with his tail between his legs, embarrassed, humiliated—and utterly guilty.

If Abram thought he'd gotten away with something, it didn't take long to discover he hadn't. In fact, he suffered several serious repercussions. He discovered the truth that would find a place in Scripture centuries later: *"The lot is cast into the lap, but its every decision is from the LORD"* (Proverbs 16:33). Or as Donald Gray Barnhouse paraphrased it: "Man throws the dice, but it's God who makes the spots come up." The spots came up in an unforgettable manner in Abram's life. He learned the hard way that God remains sovereign—despite any appearances to the contrary.

Abram faced several repercussions for his lack of faith.

First, he hurt others by his sin. He not only placed his wife in jeopardy, but he also put his servants and flocks in harm's way. Even Pharaoh and everyone who lived under his roof were in danger. Remember the well-known axiom: "Every action brings an equal and opposite reaction."[3] In Abram's case, what was true in the physical realm also had its own spiritual counterpart. Think about it: the disobedience of one man caused serious problems for scores of other people.

The same truth holds today. Disobedient, doubting Christians present a real danger to those around them. In fact, a runaway Christian poses a serious menace to others.

Remember that God had called Abram to be a blessing to others. The Lord promised that He would use Abram to bless the entire world; but it didn't happen on this day. Abram did not bring the blessing of God upon Egypt—he brought the judgment of God. He became a curse, a stench in the nostrils of Pharaoh.

How often do God's people fall into such a trap? Far too often.

Remember Achan? He was an Israelite in Joshua's day who stole money and garments from the doomed city of Jericho. He didn't dedicate them to the Lord as instructed, but hid them under his tent. And because of this one man's sin, all of Israel was defeated outside the little hamlet of Ai.

Or how about King David? He took a census of his people so that he could boast about the size of his army. Again, only one man sinned—but seventy thousand Israelites died because of his sin.

And Jonah? He tried to run away from God by booking passage on a ship headed in the opposite way God told him to go. This one man, through his sin, placed the crew and cargo of an entire ship in jeopardy. Sin rarely affects the sinner alone. Usually it entwines countless others in its deadly tentacles.

Second, Abram received a sharp rebuke from an unbeliever. Listen to the pharaoh's outraged words:

What is this you have done to me? Why did you not tell me that she was your wife? Why did you say, "She is my sister"? I might have taken her as my wife. Now therefore, here is your wife; take her and go your way. (Genesis 12:18-19)

How ironic is that? Here stands a red-faced Abram— the "man of God" and the "man of faith"—trembling before a pagan king who blasts him with a stinging (and well-deserved) rebuke.

Sometimes unbelievers have a better handle on how Christians ought to act than we do. Unbelievers actually expect Christians to be honest, faithful, trustworthy, and full of integrity. How painful it is to watch a Christian on trial who has failed before the eyes of the world. I still remember the shame I felt years ago when the media exposed Jimmy Swaggart on national television. As the world watched, *Nightline* earned one of its highest ratings. And I recall the evening that *The Tonight Show Starring Johnny Carson* exposed Peter Popoff, a televangelist and supposed faith healer, as a fake. This man claimed to receive words of wisdom and knowledge from God, when actually he had a little speaker in his ear, feeding him information about people in the audience that his wife had collected before the meeting began.

When Abram left Canaan for Egypt and lied to secure his personal safety, he got some relief from personal pressure. He did find the resources to feed his family . . . for a little while. In the end, however, it wasn't worth it. This man of God stood humiliated in front of a national, pagan audience, with nothing to say.

I once read of a man and his wife who made a visit to a local mall. In one store the man spotted a young, beautiful, curvy woman whom he stared at for a long time. When the man's wife noticed his behavior, she looked him in the eye and said, "Now, let me ask you: Was it worth it, for the trouble you're in now?"

And here's Abram, standing before Pharaoh, receiving a sharp rebuke from the angry, pagan king. You can almost hear the question: "Abram, let me ask you: Was it worth it, for all the trouble you're in now?"

Third, Abram's conduct thoroughly soiled his reputation. The Bible says, *"So Pharaoh commanded his men concerning him* [Abram]*; and they sent him away, with his wife and all that he had"* (Genesis 12:20). Can you imagine the conversation in the palace that evening?

"Can you believe that guy? What kind of 'man of God' can he be? He says he trusts in Yahweh—well, he can have that kind of faith. I hope his terrible reputation follows him wherever he goes."

(A sad note: decades later, Abraham did the same thing again, this time to another pagan king. And many years afterward, his son, Isaac, repeated the exact same sin.)

A disobedient Christian has no ability to help the lost because he's lost whatever testimony he once had. Remember what the prophet Nathan said to David after the king committed adultery with Bathsheba?

> *The LORD also has put away your sin; you shall not die. However, because by this deed you have given great occasion to the enemies of the LORD to blaspheme, the child also who is born to you shall surely die.* (2 Samuel 12:13-14).

And in a similar vein Paul wrote, *"The name of God is blasphemed among the Gentiles because of you"* (Romans 2:24).

Some years ago I talked to a man who called himself a Christian. "That's cool," I said. "I'm a Christian, too." But then he described how, as a supposed Christian, he'd broken the law, gotten busted for it, was angry that he had to go to jail, and now was trusting in the Lord to get him out of trouble.

"Do me a favor, would you?" I replied. "Don't tell anybody you're a Christian until you repent and you start following Him in righteousness. Otherwise, you're just going to give every other Christian a bad name."

Disobedient, doubting Christians with compromising lives are a menace to everyone. When doubting leads to disobedience, you become a curse to others, not a blessing. You lose your testimony.

Maybe some of us need a warning label affixed to us: "Warning: Disobedient Believer—Approach at Your Own Risk!"

Bars of Steel

Although Abram failed in this instance, difficulty in life doesn't have to lead to doubting and disobedience. In fact, we can use hardship and difficulty to our spiritual advantage and to benefit those around us.

First, when we find ourselves in difficult circumstances, ask a crucial question: "How else would I grow?" We're all going to be tested, so, like the man and his dandelions, try getting used to them. Don't expect to be immune from trials. None of us are. And if we were, we would never be of any value to God's Kingdom.

Maybe it helps to think of it like this: If you took a five-dollar bar of steel and made it into horseshoes, it would be worth about ten dollars. If you turned the same bar of steel into sewing needles, it would be worth around three-hundred-and-fifty dollars. And the same five-dollar bar of steel, made into delicate springs for watches, equals a quarter of a million dollars.

But what beating and testing it must endure to reach that high value.

Second, when our personal "Promised Land" seems difficult, we need to remain right where God put us—until God tells us to move. Stay there. I know we feel tempted to leave, to find relief somewhere else. You may think: I'm going to leave this marriage. I've got to leave this job. I have to leave this town. Don't give in to the temptation. Stay put until God shows you otherwise, either through His Word or through godly counsel. God promises you, *"Behold, I lay in Zion a stone for a foundation, a tried stone, a precious cornerstone, a sure foundation; whoever believes will not act hastily"* (Isaiah 28:16). Do you believe in Jesus? If so, then you won't act hastily. Or, as the *New Living Translation* puts it, *"Whoever believes need never run away again."*

Third, when difficulties overflow in our lives, we need to ask, "What can I learn from this?" We shouldn't be asking, "How can I get out of this?"

Hudson Taylor, the great missionary, said, "God uses men who are weak and feeble enough to lean on Him." Are you weak? Are you feeble? Then lean on Him! That's the answer.

"But it's so hard," you may say.

So lean harder. And then stay put and cast your burden upon the Lord. Tell Him, "Lord, I have a problem, and I'm making it your problem. It's yours. I need provision. And I'm trusting you. It's your move."

Put God between you and your problem. When you do, the Bible promises, *"Whoever believes on Him will not be put to shame"* (Romans 10:11).

Count on the Promises

Remember the chain saw my coworker gave me? When I looked a little closer at its box, I read some great words about the product inside:

"Engine performance system."

"Great for firewood. Great for tough jobs."

"Powerful, safer operation."

The maker promised me that—even in difficult circumstances—this new chain saw would perform well.

In a much more potent and certain way, God's promises, mixed with your faith in those promises, will make you powerful and safe even in the most difficult situations. Don't underestimate the promises God makes to you. Lean harder. Live in such a way that you will become a blessing to others, not a menace to them. And in that way, others will see your life and feel irresistibly drawn to Jesus because of what God is doing through you.

MEDITATING ON THE MARK

In this chapter we learned that Abram was also an example of doubt and disbelief. As a believer, your faith in Christ will be tested. Abram experienced three tough phases before learning to always trust in God. He failed an examination, received false confirmation, and experienced fierce repercussions.

Failed. Unless your faith is tested from time to time, it will be of no value. How has your own faith recently been tested? During this trial, how would you grade yourself based on your faith in Christ?

False. When was the last time that you were tempted to backslide and trust in the world? What reminded you that the world's peace is temporary?

Fierce. Think back to a time when a trial from God led you back to the world. What repercussions did your unfaith bring to you?

MODELING THE MASTER'S MARK

Failed. 1 Corinthians 10:13: *"No temptation has overtaken you except such as is common to man; but God is faithful, who will not allow you to be tempted beyond what you are able, but with the temptation will also make the way of escape, that you may be able to bear it."*

False. John 14:27: *"Peace I leave with you, My peace I give to you; not as the world gives do I give to you."*

Fierce. Proverbs 16:25: *"There is a way that seems right to a man, but its end is the way of death."*

MAKING YOUR MARK

Make a list of three promises of God that you most need to rely on today. Carry these three promises with you throughout the week and commit them to memory.

CHAPTER FOUR

Two Men Under One Microscope

Several years ag, a wealthy Chinese businessman visited America and became fascinated with microscopes. He bought one, took it home, and loved to look at flowers, crystals, hair—anything, really. One night he decided to place some of the rice he loved to eat under the microscope. He was shocked to discover microorganisms teeming over his favorite food. It devastated him because he loved rice. Confronted with this new information, he had to do something. So he did.

He took the microscope out of his house and smashed it to pieces.

We're going to take two men, Abram and Lot, and place them both under God's microscope. We'll compare their lives and we'll also compare ourselves to them, to discover which of the two we most resemble. As we make these comparisons, we'll find ourselves under the microscope. And we'll probably see some things we may not like. Give yourself an honest evaluation—but don't smash the microscope.

Choices

People who make their mark on the world learn from their mistakes. And people who fail to learn from their mistakes don't make their mark. In Genesis 13, Abram learned from his mistakes and grew in faith and spiritual maturity. But we'll see another man, Lot, who failed to learn and kept messing up.

Who do you think made a bigger mark on the world?

This is the story of two close relatives. But while they were related physically, they were hardly related to each other spiritually. Abram was a spiritual man; he was far from perfect, but he was back in Canaan and wiser because of his mistakes in Egypt. Lot was a more worldly man—he set his sights on material things. So what made the difference between them?

Choices.

Someone once said, "We make our choices and then our choices make us." One little choice can change the course of history. One little decision can change nations, families, and individuals.

A courthouse in the Midwest is so situated on a hill that raindrops falling on one side of its roof go down into the streams, into a river, through the Great Lakes, and end up in the Atlantic Ocean. Raindrops falling on the other side of the building make their way down the other side of the hill into the Ohio River, then the Mississippi River, and into the Gulf of Mexico. Just a little bit of wind makes all the difference as to the destination of those raindrops.

It's the same with our choices. We make decisions that yield tremendous ramifications for years and decades to come—even into eternity. These choices ultimately determine where we end up.

As we compare the lives of Abram and Lot, we will look at four points of acute difference. I think you will see how the choices of these men determined their very different legacies.

A Root

When Abram left Egypt, he took his family and all his possessions and headed back to the place where he had set up his tents when he first arrived in Canaan, between Bethel and Ai. He made a beeline for the altar he set up earlier and called upon the name of the Lord.

Abram's nephew, Lot, followed along behind his uncle, along with his own herds and flocks. Lot was the son of Haran, Abram's brother, who died in Ur. Ever since Haran died, it appears that Lot looked up to Abram as a sort of father figure—an example to follow. So Lot followed his uncle all the way from Ur to Haran, from Haran into Canaan, from Canaan to Egypt, and then back again to Canaan. Both men were wealthy.

In the Bible, having riches is presented as neither a necessarily good thing nor a bad thing; it's a neutral thing. It all depends on how you use those riches. Some of God's greatest servants had money. Some used it well and wisely; some didn't.

Someone is probably thinking: the Bible said that money is the root of all evil.

I'm not sure what Bible you're reading. The Scripture says, *"For the love of money is a root of all kinds of evil"* (1 Timothy 6:10, emphasis mine). You can be poor and love money, and the results will devastate you. But sometimes God blesses somebody financially, and they use the money to bless others and further God's Kingdom. The Bible says, *"Through wisdom a house is built, and by understanding it is established; by knowledge the rooms are filled with all precious and pleasant riches"* (Proverbs 24:3-4). But "pleasant riches" can become quite a problem for many of us.

Here's the crucial difference between the two men: while Abram possessed riches, riches possessed Lot. Abram used his wealth for good; Lot's wealth drove him to one bad decision after another. Both men left Egypt and returned to Canaan, but with one major difference: Abraham repented; Lot just returned.

After their return:

> Lot lifted up his eyes and saw all the plain of Jordan, that it was well watered everywhere (before the LORD destroyed Sodom and Gomorrah) like the garden of the LORD, like the land of Egypt as you go up toward Zoar. (Genesis 13:10)

Lot may have left Egypt—but Egypt never left him. When Lot saw the plain of Jordan, he said, "Oh, that looks a lot like Egypt. I want that land, because I miss Egypt. I've gotta have it!" Egypt had become his frame of reference.

We all have a frame of reference from which we make comparisons. Usually they're based on where we were born and raised or where we spent a lot of time. But these comparisons aren't always fair.

I grew up in southern California, so that's my frame of reference. Sometimes I drive my wife nuts with my comparisons. It'll be a nice, balmy, summer afternoon in Albuquerque and I'll say, "Oh, this is like California." Or we'll drive through a neighborhood and see houses that resemble those on the West Coast and I'll say, "This neighborhood looks like something you'd see back in California." Or we'll go to a lake and I'll say, "Boy, this is nice water, but it's not the Pacific." On the other hand, we might be driving down the freeway, get caught in traffic, and I'll say, "Boy, the traffic is horrible"—and my wife will smile, cut me off, and say, "But not as bad as California."

In a similar way, Egypt became Lot's frame of reference. That's what he wanted to duplicate in Canaan.

Now, before I take anyone too far in the wrong direction, I should say that the New Testament presents a much more positive picture of Lot. Peter calls him "righteous Lot." (See 2 Peter 2:7.) Lot was grieved by all the evil going on in Sodom, but I think Peter calls him "righteous" simply in comparison to all the wickedness of Sodom and Gomorrah. We never read of Lot building an altar, we never read of Lot worshiping, and we never read of Lot praying.

In this example we also see God's amazing grace at work. I find it remarkable that the New Testament never mentions any of the sins of the Old Testament saints. It doesn't recall David's adultery, Abraham's lapses in faith, Samson's dalliances with Delilah, Noah's getting drunk, and on and on. We read all about these sordid incidents in the Old Testament, but you'll look in vain for them in the New Testament. It's almost as if God has forgotten them—which is exactly what He promises to do in Hebrews 10:17—*"Their sins and their lawless deeds I will remember no more."*

As we study the profiles of these two men, it seems that while Abram walked with God, Lot walked with Abram. Abram was a friend of God; Lot was a friend of Abram.

A lot of people follow Lot's example, trying to tag along with believing relatives. They never make their own stand for Christ. They try to live off somebody else's faith, somebody else's commitment to Christ. Maybe they grew up in church, but they really love the world. So they tag along—and that's a dangerous position to take. It's a perilous profile to have.

Recall what James wrote: *"Do you not know that friendship with the world is enmity with God?"* (James 4:4). If your whole aim is to enjoy this world, then you can't be God's friend. Lot appears to lean upon Abram's faith rather than leaning upon the Lord. But God has no grandchildren. He has children—a direct relationship with each individual.

You can't say, "Well, my father and grandmother were faithful, churchgoing people." Okay, but what about you? How's your own relationship with Christ?

When Abram returned to Canaan, he immediately called on the name of the Lord. This man had learned his lesson. He had had enough of Egypt. He came back to the land of promise, repented of his past, and started doing again what he did at the beginning. That sounds a lot like the passage in Revelation where Jesus wrote to the members of the church at Ephesus, who had left their first love. He told them, *"Remember therefore from where you have fallen; repent and do the first works"* (Revelation 2:5). That's the open door for anyone who has drifted from God. You go back to the beginning, to your original place of devotion and worship. That's what Abram did—that's repentance.

A lot of Christians—mistakenly—think repentance is for unbelievers only: "Yeah, they're heathens; they need to repent." Let's be honest: God convicts us of a lot of things that call for repentance. It's an ongoing process as He reveals more and more of himself.

In their book *Sold Out!*, Richard Ganz and William Edgar wrote, "Churches want to hear nice, optimistic messages free of the mention of sin or a call for repentance. Churches want nice, lean programming directed at nice, clean families, leading to growth without sacrifice. They want their organization to become bigger and bigger even as their God becomes smaller and smaller."

That's Lot—but it's definitely not Abram. Their profiles reveal two totally different kinds of men.

Stuff

Soon after Abram and Lot returned from Egypt, they ran into a sticky situation. Since both men had large flocks and herds, they simply couldn't live in the same place. The land could not support both of them at the same time. They learned of the predicament through their herdsmen, who started fighting turf wars.

Most of us can relate to such a predicament. We don't realize we have so much stuff until we move. And then we look inside the boxes and say, "When did we collect all this stuff?" And if we pack it and move it, trust me, we won't see it again until we move the next time. That's the rub with having stuff: the more we have, the more we have to manage. And that can provide fertile ground for conflict.

A few years ago we moved into the mountains and began looking through our stuff. I'm very pragmatic when it comes to stuff—especially other people's stuff. I throw it away. It's just clogging up the garage, so I figure, let's get rid of it. So I started trashing some stuff.

"Hey, what are you doing with that box?"

"I'm throwing it away."

"But that's my stuff!"

Abram and Lot had a "stuff" problem. But their predicament went a little deeper than throwing out boxes. The Bible says, *"The Canaanites and the Perizzites then dwelt in the land"* (Genesis 13:7). Why would Moses include this detail? He was trying to show us a couple of things. First, he wanted us to know that these two men faced competition not merely from each other, but from the people who lived there first. Second, he wanted to remind us that unbelievers overhear our family quarrels. The world was watching Abram and Lot.

The world watches what we do and listens to what we say, doesn't it? It does very closely. In fact, it's a surprise when an unbeliever tells us something he's noticed about us—we didn't even know he was looking. But we are under the microscope.

Centuries ago the famed sculptor Michelangelo and the great painter Rafael were hired to decorate the Vatican.

The celebrated artists worked as everyone watched—but eventually a rivalry broke out. The enmity became so heated that they refused to speak to one another when they passed in the hallway. And everybody knew it. The ironic thing is, they were doing it all "for the glory of God"—as the entire world looked on. How sad.

The Best

When Abram learned of the conflict between his herdsmen and Lot's, he told his nephew to choose whatever part of the land he wanted. If Lot went to the right, Abram would go to the left.

As the oldest, Abram should have had first choice. But he wanted to be a peacemaker, not a troublemaker, so he told Lot he'd take whatever Lot didn't want. Remember, God had promised Abram the whole land—but gracious Abram preferred peace rather than trouble.

So Abram demonstrated his preference to live out the New Testament instructions we know so well:

> *Let nothing be done through selfish ambition or conceit, but in lowliness of mind let each of you esteem others better than himself. Let each of you look out not only for his own interests, but also for the interests of others.* (Philippians 2:3-4)

Abram looked to the interests of Lot and gave him first choice.

And what did Lot choose?

> *Then Lot chose for himself all the plain of Jordan, and Lot journeyed east. And they separated from each other. Abram dwelt in the land of Canaan, and Lot dwelt in the cities of the plain and pitched his*

tent even as far as Sodom. But the men of Sodom were exceedingly wicked and sinful against the LORD. (Genesis 13:11-13)

Lot chose the Jordan plain because it looked good to him. Here was a man driven completely by his senses. He did what he thought best for him, based solely on his outward observations. He lifted his eyes and "saw." Literally the word means, "he looked with longing."

Doesn't that sound a lot like Eve? In the Garden of Eden, she looked at the one prohibited tree and "... saw that the tree was good for food, that it was pleasant to the eyes, and a tree desirable to make one wise, she took of its fruit and ate" (Genesis 3:6). The eyes will always see what the heart loves. John said, "For all that is in the world—the lust of the flesh, the lust of the eyes, and the pride of life—is not of the Father but is of the world" (1 John 2:16).

The Apostle Paul said that—as believers—we walk by faith and not by sight. (See 2 Corinthians 5:7.) But Lot walked by sight rather than by faith. Lot made his choice based upon what looked best to him materially—not spiritually. "Oh, I want the Jordan plain! There's nothing like it. It's the best. Move over, Abe."

In 1971, gunmen looted a bank in London and stole seven million dollars worth of goods. Part of their heist included a box of jewelry worth five hundred thousand dollars.[1] The victimized woman wailed when she heard about the theft. "My whole life was in that box!" she moaned. What a sad statement. Her whole life was in that box? One day we'll all end up in another box—and if all our life is in there, it will be a sad day, indeed.

Lot would say, "My whole life is Sodom. It's out on the plain and it looks so good." Lot made his choices by considering the material opportunities. But it wouldn't last long.

How do you make your choices? Upon what do you base those choices? What process do you use for deciding things in life—where you'll go, what you'll do, where you'll live? Do you make your decisions based primarily on material considerations or on spiritual realities?

Bible commentator Griffith Thomas wrote:

> Even professedly Christian people often choose their home in a locality simply for its scenery or society or its other material advantages without once inquiring, 'What church opportunities are there?' The souls of their children may starve among worldliness and polite indifference.

Not Abram. Abram didn't walk by sight. He walked by his faith in the promises of God.

Lot said, "I want the best of the land." Abram replied, "Go for it." Abram didn't know it, but God was about to give him something better: himself, as well as ironclad promises for Abram's descendants.

The writer of Hebrews said:

> *By faith he* [Abraham] *dwelt in the land of promise as in a foreign country, dwelling in tents with Isaac and Jacob, the heirs with him of the same promise; for he waited for the city which has foundations, whose builder and maker is God.* (Hebrews 11:9-10)

No geography on Earth matters as much as the will of God. It doesn't matter if you live here or there, because you're just passing through. You should be moving toward a heavenly city. And the best deal isn't what you find down here. The best deal is what's up ahead—and Abram knew it.

Do you?

Separate

After Lot chose for himself the plain of the Jordan, God told Abram:

> *Lift your eyes now and look from the place where you are—northward, southward, eastward, and westward; for all the land which you see I give to you and your descendants forever. And I will make your descendants as the dust of the earth; so that if a man could number the dust of the earth, then your descendants also could be numbered. Arise, walk in the land through its length and its width, for I give it to you.* (Genesis 13:14-17)

When Abram heard this magnificent promise, he *"... moved his tent, and went and dwelt by the terebinth trees of Mamre, which are in Hebron, and built an altar there to the LORD"* (Genesis 13:18). Lot thought he'd gotten the better deal. He looked up and saw the fertile plain of the Jordan and all that it could offer him. He looked to the richness of the Earth. But soon afterward God spoke to Abram and said, "Hey, Abe! Lift up your eyes and see what I have to offer you."

In separating, the two men illustrated a vital biblical principle: *"Can two walk together, unless they are agreed?"* (Amos 3:3). This pair did not agree. In terms of the goals of their lives, they were heading in two opposite directions. This separation was beneficial for Abram, but not so for Lot.

Years before, God told Abram, "Leave your father's house." He dragged his feet and didn't obey immediately; in fact, Abram brought Dad and Lot and everything else with him. When he finally left for Canaan, Lot still remained with him. But now the time for separation had come—and only then did Abram's life really begin to blossom.

God often tells us to make separations. He tells us to separate from worldly behavior and lifestyles. (See 1 Peter 2:1-4.) He tells us to separate from ungodly associates (see 2 Corinthians 6:17 and 1 Corinthians 15:33). Why does He give us these instructions? We know that certain people can drag us down spiritually and hinder our spiritual growth. We've all been around such individuals. Stick around them too long and you feel exhausted, worn out, and dragged down. Certain people diminish your spiritual appetite. They may profess to be Christians, but when you're around them, it seems like they have no real heart for God or prayer. They show far more interest in worldly things, worldly events, and worldly activities. They complain, they murmur, they gripe, they backbite, they gossip. After one night of hanging out with them, you feel as though a dead weight is hanging from your neck. So you separate.

On the other hand, being around godly people gives you a stronger appetite for spiritual things. They inspire you to grow. A verse from the New Testament sums it up well: *"Flee also youthful lusts; but pursue righteousness, faith, love, peace with those who call on the Lord out of a pure heart"* (2 Timothy 2:22). That's what Abram did. He separated from Lot. And in response, God declared His firm intent to bless Abram.

After the separation, Lot moved on to what looked like a place of blessing—but where Lot went, Abram had no desire to go. Lot took a number of steps downward:

Step One: Lot was driven by his senses.

Step Two: Lot separated from a man of godly spiritual influence.

Step Three: Lot pitched his tent toward Sodom, on the border of a wicked city.

Step Four: Lot moved into Sodom.

Step Five: Lot became a politician in Sodom.

Imagine if you were there and could ask Lot some tough questions: "What are you doing? Don't you know this city stinks; that it's sinful?"

"I can handle it, dude," he might have said. "Don't worry about me. Worry about what's going on in your own life. Don't judge me, man, I can handle it." He would probably talk about all the advantages the city had to offer him and his family.

Although in the end Lot "sat at the gate" of the city—meaning he reached a place of great influence and notoriety—he didn't influence the city for good. Instead, it dragged him down. You could look at Lot's life and sum it up with Psalm 1:

Blessed is the man who walks not in the counsel of the ungodly, nor stands in the path of sinners, nor sits in the seat of the scornful; but his delight is in the law of the LORD. (Psalm 1:1-2a)

While Lot delighted in the green grass of the Jordan valley, Abram delighted in the promises of God. And in the end—that choice made all the difference.

Be Careful

Looking at the differences between Abram and Lot, we reach three conclusions:

First, be careful of your vision. Be careful how you see material things and how you look at your life. How do you view it? Lot viewed the world only. He looked up and saw stuff. Abram looked up and kept looking up. He saw God. You might say that Lot looked down before he looked up, while Abram looked up before he looked down. Be careful of your vision.

Second, be careful of your values. Lot had a tent, but no altar. Abram had a tent and an altar; but in his life, the altar took precedence. That was his priority, his value system. Be careful of your values.

Third, be careful of your choices. Treat each choice—no matter how small it may appear—as a powerful thing. It could have enormous consequences. Remember what Lot chose and what he lost. And consider what Abram chose and what he received. Be careful of your choices.

Arnold Schwarzenegger announced his plans to run for governor of the state of California while appearing on Jay Leno's TV show. Drawing on his enormous Hollywood connections and popular action-movie background, in classic style he told his audience, "I have one message for the politicians: If you don't do your job, it's *hasta la vista*, baby." Most of us watching the show thought that if he failed in his first attempt (he didn't, of course), he'd use his most famous line: "I'll be back."

When Abram found himself and his family in the middle of a famine, he said *hasta la vista* to the land of Canaan. But after surviving the subsequent disaster in Egypt, he said, "I'll be back." And so Abram returned to the land of promise, back to the altar, back to the promises of God.

It's never too late for any of us.

Grass or Grace?

Two men. Two lives. Two very different sets of values. One wanted the altar of God; the other wanted the allurements of the world. One felt driven by the promises of God; the other was driven by his senses.

Look at it this way: while Lot got grass for his cows, Abram got grace for his kids. At the time, of course, Abram didn't have any children, but one day he would. In fact, God promised he'd have so many descendants that he wouldn't be able to count them all.

Lot made his choices based on his ideas of how best to care for his wife and children. "This is the best choice for my family," he might have said. Unfortunately, in the end he'd lose almost his entire family—all because he didn't place God first.

Abram simply said, "I'll let God choose for me." And in response, God promised to give him a family so big he wouldn't know what to do with it.

It is always better to let God choose for you. Regard little choices like the raindrops that fall on that Midwestern courthouse. "Little" choices can have tremendous consequences.

Have you ever heard the famous comparison between the legacies of Max Jukes and Jonathan Edwards? Jukes lived in New York during the eighteenth century and did not believe in Christ or in Christian training. He refused to take his children to church, even when they asked to go. Of his 1,026 descendants, 300 were sent to prison for an average term of thirteen years; 190 became prostitutes; 680 were admitted alcoholics. His family cost the government in excess of $420,000.

Jonathan Edwards, on the other hand, lived in New England at the same time as Jukes. He loved the Lord and saw that his children were in church every Sunday. He served the Lord to the best of his ability. Of his 929 descendants, 430 became ministers; eighty-six became university professors; thirteen became university presidents; seventy-five authored good books; seven were elected to the U.S. Congress; and one became vice president of the United States. His family never cost the state one cent, but contributed immeasurably to the economy and the well-being of the country. Which would you choose?

Jukes or Edwards?

Lot or Abram?

As we've looked at Abram and Lot—and ourselves—under the microscope, what has God been showing you? Is He calling you to repent, to remember from where you have fallen, and to return and do your first works all over again? Or have you been trying to tag along with "religious" members of your family and haven't yet personally committed yourself to Christ? Maybe, like Lot, you've been gazing longingly at the stuff of the world and God is saying to you, "Child, come home. Be mine."

Jukes or Edwards? Lot or Abram? It's your choice. But what a difference that choice makes.

MEDITATING ON THE MARK

In this chapter we learned that people who truly make a mark learn from their mistakes. In fact, comparing Abram and Lot, we see that the distinction came down to the choices they made. The two were different in four ways: profile, predicament, preference, and provision.

Profile. Abram possessed riches, but riches possessed Lot. With whom do you most identify? How can you take steps to lessen the control that worldly riches exert over you?

Predicament. When have you been at odds with another believer? An unbeliever? Did you handle the difficulty in a godly manner in both situations?

Preference. Think about some important choices you've made: where to live, whom to marry, what vehicle to drive. How many of these choices were based on what "looked good"?

Provision. Are there people in your life who are hindering your spiritual growth? Think on ways to remove such distractions and keep them from dragging you down.

MODELING THE MASTER'S MARK

Profile. Ecclesiastes 5:10: *"He who loves silver will not be satisfied with silver; nor he who loves abundance, with increase."*

Predicament. Matthew 5:9: *"Blessed are the peacemakers, for they shall be called sons of God."*

Preference. 1 Samuel 16:7: *"For the LORD does not see as man sees; for man looks at the outward appearance, but the LORD looks at the heart."*

Provision. 2 Corinthians 6:14: *"Do not be unequally yoked together with unbelievers. For what fellowship has righteousness with lawlessness? And what communion has light with darkness?"*

MAKING YOUR MARK

Do you remember when you first came to Christ? Resolve today to be in prayer to refresh that initial excitement, and redo what you did at your born-again beginning.

CHAPTER FIVE

The Glimmer of the Godly in a Cauldron of Crisis

Heat seems to bring out the worst in people—as well as the best. A few years ago, the electric grid in the northeastern United States went out, bringing out the worst in a few folks. There were several reports of broken windows and looting. But it also brought out the best.

Although millions of people lost electrical power in the midst of sweltering temperatures, officials were astonished that the vast majority of men and women remained kind, considerate, and even helpful. Some folks emptied their refrigerators and invited neighbors to eat their food in the street. Because of this, they got to meet men and women, boys and girls—neighbors they had never known. In places like Boston and New York City, people went stargazing, an activity many of them had never enjoyed before because of light pollution.

Heat has similar effects on corn. If you put normal corn in a four-hundred-degree pan, it will wither, shrivel, and become hard. But put popcorn in the same pan at the same temperature and the heat causes the gases within the kernels to expand. And we know the rest of the delicious story—the popcorn expands several times its original size and becomes a delightful treat.

That's often how adversity works. Some people, in the heat of adversity, become hardened and shriveled; others become enlarged by it, bettered by it, and bless others because of it. What makes the difference? It's not the trials; they're the same for both groups. What makes the difference is the way each group responds to the trials.

Shimmering in the Heat

Genesis 14 tells the story of an international crisis. Abram's nephew, Lot, was captured by an alliance of ancient superpowers. That crisis moved Abram to action. He became enlarged and stronger during this heated time. In fact, he came through it shining.

We should probably compare Abram to gold rather than to popcorn. Just as impurities are skimmed off the top of gold heated to the melting point, this man glimmered in a cauldron of crisis. But note this: the shimmering lit up this man only during a time of intense trial.

Peter wrote:

> *In this you greatly rejoice, though now for a little while, if need be, you have been grieved by various trials, that the genuineness of your faith, being much more precious than gold that perishes, though it is tested by fire, may be found to praise, honor, and glory at the revelation of Jesus Christ.* (1 Peter 1:6-7)

Just as fire tests and purifies gold, so adversity tests and has the potential to purify believers.

Abram came through this test glistening.

If we want to make our mark on the world, at some point we must ask ourselves, "How do growing, godly people of faith respond in a time of crisis?"

When your daughter, whom you told, "Don't date that guy; he's trouble," dates him anyway—and ends up pregnant—how do you respond?

When that son of yours squanders his college fund on some worthless purchase that he just "had" to have, how do you respond?

When your business partner invests all of the company's money in Florida swampland and loses everything, how do you respond?

Do you blow up? Do you get angry and say, "I told you so"? Do you gloat? Or do you take a different tack?

Abram chose that different tack. In a time of great crisis, he embodied five glimmering qualities that people of faith should always exhibit when troubles come.

As we look at the crisis in Abram's life, ask yourself what kind of friends you want around when you go through a crisis. And ask what kind of friend you want to be when your friends face crises of their own.

First Glimmering Quality: Sympathy

In the first war recorded in the Bible, Abram demonstrated sympathy for his wayward nephew, Lot. Sympathy is very often the first quality that godly people reveal in a crisis.

An earlier war pitted four kings against five. Four powers from the east formed a coalition headed up by a king named Chedorlaomer. They all came from the area where Abraham grew up, Mesopotamia and the Euphrates River valley. They swept through the land, defeating the forces of five city-states around the area of the Sea of Galilee and the Dead Sea—the eastern portion of modern Israel, including Sodom and Gomorrah. After the invaders conquered those five city-states, the victorious kings placed them under tribute for twelve years.

In year thirteen, the five defeated rulers said, "We've had enough; we're going to rebel." They did, but unsuccessfully. Their rebellion quickly aroused the wrath of the four opposing superpowers, who once more swept through the desert region, plundering and killing and taking captive a host of innocent people. One of those captives was Lot.

When Abram heard what had happened to his nephew, he acted immediately. He armed the 318 trained servants who had been born in his house and pursued the kings "as far as Dan." (See Genesis 14:14.) Now, it would have been easy for Abram to say, "Hmmm, isn't that interesting? Lot made his bed; now he can lie in it. It serves him right! He chose to pitch his tent toward Sodom. He got what was coming to him." However, Abram didn't do that; instead, his immediate response demonstrated great sympathy for his nephew. He cared deeply for Lot and quickly mobilized his resources to do something to help.

From an historical perspective, this is unusual. Sympathy, grace, and mercy simply did not rank high within ancient kingdoms, especially those at war. One Roman historian-philosopher even said, "Mercy is a disease of the soul and the ultimate sign of weakness."[1] That's why stories of the ancient world overflow with accounts of intrigue, revenge, and cruelty—not sympathy, mercy, or rescue.

But Abram is not typical. Touched by Lot's plight, he acts decisively.

Have attitudes changed a great deal since ancient times? You might think so. We might flatter ourselves and say that we've grown more merciful, more gracious, and more willing to help those with acute needs.

Not necessarily so.

Human nature seems perfectly willing to let those who have made a mistake stew in the consequences—or even worse. Consider an excerpt from the Satanic bible, a vile remake of the Beatitudes: "Hate your enemies with a whole heart," it says. "And if a man smite you on one cheek, smash him on the other. Smite him hip and thigh, for self-preservation is the highest law. Stop the way of them that would persecute you, let them be as chaff before the cyclone. And after they have fallen, rejoice in thine own salvation. Cursed are the weak, for they shall inherit the yoke. Cursed are the righteously humble, for they shall be trodden under cloven hooves."[2]

If Abram had adopted such an evil mentality, Lot wouldn't have had a chance. But the godly act differently than the ungodly in a time of crisis. When wars or famines break out around the world, who usually acts first? Generally, it's Christians. Others may feel sympathy for the afflicted, but when a crisis calls for food or medicine or immediate response, history shows that followers of Christ, or nations influenced by Christians, tend to respond first.

How did Nehemiah react when he heard about the suffering of his fellow Israelites in Jerusalem? He wept and then he acted.

What did Jeremiah do when he saw Jerusalem ravaged by the Babylonians? Did he say, "Well, I prophesied the destruction"? No, he wept.

What did Jesus do when He looked over the city of Jerusalem, knowing its citizens would reject Him and that the Romans would later obliterate the city? He wept for them.

Jesus Christ is the ultimate man of sympathy. He is a *"Man of sorrows and acquainted with grief"* (Isaiah 53:3). When He saw the hungry crowd in Galilee, the Bible says He *"was moved with compassion for them, because they were weary and scattered, like sheep having no shepherd"* (Matthew 9:36). The words "moved with compassion" translates to the Greek word *splonkna*, which literally means "intestines." Ancient people equated the deepest emotional part of a person to the gut. Today we might say, "I love you with all my heart," but they would say, "I love you with all my intestines." To feel deeply was to feel something deep inside the gut. The idea is the expression of compassion and sympathy.

Jesus also said, *"Blessed are the merciful, for they shall themselves obtain mercy"* (Matthew 5:7). One of the greatest attributes of Jesus that a Christian can emulate is to become a person of mercy, sympathy, and compassion. Paul put it this way: *"Brethren, if a man is overtaken in any trespass, you who are spiritual restore such a one in a spirit of gentleness, considering yourself lest you also be tempted"* (Galatians 6:1).

Is sympathy one of your attributes? When something bad happens to someone, do you immediately respond with, "How may I help?" With great poignancy, Henry Drummond once asked, "How many prodigals are kept out of the Kingdom of God by those unlovely characters who profess to be inside?"

Abram moved quickly to rescue Lot. He showed his sympathy.

Second Glimmering Quality: Bravery

We've already seen Abram as a man of faith and as a man of peace, but through this incident we begin to see a whole new side of him. We see him with lion-like courage, arming his servants and going to war against a far superior force.

Proverbs 28:1 reads: *"The wicked flee when no one pursues, but the righteous are bold as a lion."* Abram took 318 of his servants, along with three Amorite allies, and pursued the attackers into the far north. *"He divided his forces against them by night, and he and his servants attacked them and pursued them as far as Hobah, which is north of Damascus"* (Genesis 14:15). Abram had a large staff but a very small army, especially against a federation of four superpowers. But there he and his men were—armed, dangerous, and ready to fight.

They were brave men, but also wise ones. They knew they couldn't defeat such a superior force under normal circumstances, so they decided, "Let's do something when it's dark. Let's divide our forces for a nighttime ambush." That took bravery.

True sympathy begets bravery, because people who know their God know what God would do in a time of crisis, and so they endeavor to act like Him: *"The people who know their God shall be strong, and carry out great exploits"* (Daniel 11:32).

Think of Gideon and his 300 men attacking the Midianite army—that's a great exploit. Think of the little shepherd boy named David fighting a nine-foot giant named Goliath—that's a great exploit.

Think of Joshua and Caleb saying, "Let's take the land. The giants? We'll eat them for lunch." That's a great exploit. All made possible because they knew their God.

When did others last see your bravery? When did you last feel moved with compassion and then act upon it? When was the last time you dared to emerge from behind the hallowed walls of your church, take an assessment of the needy, hurting people around you, and say, "I am moved with compassion for them and I'm going to do something about it"? The homeless, the hungry, the tiny infants slaughtered in abortion clinics, teenagers on drugs, adults who need a helping hand—when did you last act on your compassion and show your bravery?

Remember what Jesus said:

"I was hungry and you gave Me food; I was thirsty and you gave Me drink; I was a stranger and you took Me in; I was naked and you clothed Me; I was sick and you visited Me; I was in prison and you came to Me." Then the righteous will answer Him, saying, "Lord, when did we see You hungry and feed You, or thirsty and give You drink? When did we see You a stranger and take You in, or naked and clothe You? Or when did we see You sick, or in prison, and come to You?" (Matthew 25:35-39)

And He will respond, *"Inasmuch as you did it to one of the least of these My brethren, you did it to Me"* (Matthew 25:40).

There's a story told of a homeless lady who asked a local church for help, but the church wanted nothing to do with her. She wrote a note back to the vicar of the parish. "I was hungry, and you formed a humanities group to discuss my hunger," she wrote. "I was imprisoned, and you crept off quietly to your chapel and prayed for my release. I was naked, and in your mind you debated the morality of my appearance. I was sick, and you knelt and thanked God for your health. I was homeless, and you preached to me of the spiritual shelter of the love of God. I was lonely, and you left me alone to pray for me. You seemed so holy, so close to God—but I am still very hungry and lonely and cold."[3]

As soon as Abram heard of Lot's plight, he declared, "I have to do something about this." So he armed his servants, accepted help from his allies, and they all went to help. Sympathy begets bravery.

Notice that Abram had weapons with him. Notice also that he trained his 318 servants in the art of warfare. Abram was a man of peace, but he was also a wise man who must have thought, *I'm a nomad traveling through this land. At some point, we may have to get involved in a war. I had better be prepared for that day. I love peace enough to fight for it.*

Abram put himself—and his life—on the line.

Jesus said, *"Greater love has no one than this, than to lay down one's life for his friends"* (John 15:13). Abram, the man of faith, was no pacifist. When the situation called for it, he acted as a man of war.

Francis Schaeffer once said, "I am not a pacifist, because pacifism in the fallen world in which we live means we must desert the very people that deserve our greatest help." And then he gave an example.

"Imagine you're walking down the street," he said, "and you see this big thug beating up on a helpless little girl. What do you do? What does love mean to you at that time, at that moment? Well, you'd probably go over to him and try to negotiate.

"'Excuse me, big mean bully, but please don't do that. Let's sit down and talk.'

"Well, that's good, but what if he decides not to? What if he pays no attention to you but keeps beating her up mercilessly? What does love mean to you then? It had better mean that you will do anything it takes to stop that thug, including putting him out of life."

Abram drew on his bravery and moved quickly to rescue his captive nephew.

Third Glimmering Quality: Capability

When you match compassion and bravery with capability, you can make a tremendous mark on your world. The Bible tells us that Abram *"divided his forces against them by night, and he and his servants attacked them and pursued them as far as Hobah, which is north of Damascus. So he brought back all the goods, and also brought back his brother Lot and his goods, as well as the women and the people"* (Genesis 14:15-16).

Notice some the phrases used to describe Abram's actions: He "attacked," he "pursued," and he "brought back" both the spoils and the captives. Here was a man who—with strategy, teamwork, and a sense of persistence— chased the large pagan armies one hundred and fifty miles north of where he began. He didn't just say, "I'm going to scare them away, and then it'll be done." He continued to fight until he had completed the job.

That's capability.

Whenever you feel moved to do something in the will of God and you go for it, you may not get instant success. You might have to work at it for days or weeks or months or even years to see any results. Charles Spurgeon once said, "By perseverance the snail reached the ark." I've thought about that. I picture this crazy menagerie of animals going into the ark. Giraffes with their huge steps didn't take long. Horses galloped in; cheetahs sprinted in. But the snails? Maybe they started out first, but by persistence they kept going and going until they reached the ark.

Martin Luther nailed ninety-five theses on the Wittenberg door in Germany. He didn't see change overnight—it took years to see real transformation occur in the Church.

Wilbur and Orville Wright decided, "We want to fly." People responded, "You guys are idiots." Their own father said, "Flight is reserved for the birds and the angels. It's blasphemy to think you could fly." But they tried, failed, kept at it, and persisted, until one day they accomplished what they had set out to do.

Winston Churchill delivered his most famous speech in 1941 to his alma mater, the Harlow School in Great Britain. At that time, all of Europe felt the devastating effects of World War II. Churchill said his nation entered the war unprepared, but then worked to become prepared. So Churchill gave a little speech to the students of that school—and also to his entire war-torn nation. He concluded by saying, "Never give in. Never give in. Never, never, never, never. In nothing, great or small, large or petty, never give in except to convictions of honor and good sense. Never yield to force, never yield to the apparently overwhelming might of the enemy."

If your sympathy moves you to brave action, then hang in there until you get victory. That's what Abram did, and because of it he made a tremendous mark on his world.

Fourth Glimmering Quality: Integrity

When Abram returned home from his unlikely victory, a giddy king of Sodom hurried out to meet him. He told Abram to keep all the goods he had recaptured, but to return to him the freed hostages. Here's how Abram responded:

> *I have raised my hand to the LORD, God Most High, the Possessor of heaven and earth, that I will take nothing, from a thread to a sandal strap, and that I will not take anything that is yours, lest you should say, "I have made Abram rich"—except only what the young men have eaten, and the portion of the men who went with me: Aner, Eschcol, and Mamre; let them take their portion.* (Genesis 14:22-24)

Why did Abram refuse the king's handsome offer of reward? According to Abram, he had sworn an oath to God before the battle that he would not keep any of the goods he might recover. He probably said something like this to God: "God, you give me the victory, and I'll give you all the glory. I won't take anything for myself. I don't need the money; you've already given me more than I need. So I promise to give you all the glory."

Now, why would Abram make such a vow? He knew that if God gave him success and he kept the recovered goods for himself, people would say, "Oh, I know why Abram did this. I know why he went to war. He did it for the money. He knew that Bera, the king of Sodom, would reward him." Since Abram knew that a report like that would seemingly diminish the glory of God, he refused any material reward from the king.

At this point we start dealing with the slippery area of motives. Why do you do what you do? Why do you get involved in ministry? Do you do it for fame or notoriety? Do you do it so others will notice you? So that maybe you'll get offered a position on staff? Or do you say, "I'm doing this purely for the glory of God"?

Abram acted as he did to rescue Lot—and to give God all the glory.

Abram's attitude reminds me of George Beverly Shea's song, "I'd Rather Have Jesus."

> *I'd rather have Jesus than silver or gold;*
> *I'd rather be His than have riches untold;*
> *I'd rather have Jesus than houses or lands,*
> *I'd rather be led by His nail pierced hands. . . .*
> *Than to be the king of a vast domain*
> *Or be held in sin's dread sway,*
> *I'd rather have Jesus than anything*
> *This world affords today.*[4]

This is where integrity comes into play. Abram said something to God before the battle, and afterward he followed through. Do you know what integrity means? It means keeping your promise. It means doing what you said you'd do.

In a book he wrote on integrity, Ted Engstrom looked around the Christian community and noticed that many Christians have a form of AIDS—in this case, **A**cquired **I**ntegrity **D**eficiency **S**yndrome. They say certain things and make broad promises, but they don't keep either their word or their promises.[5]

Every time a husband leaves his wife or a wife leaves her husband; every time a pastor gets involved in a scandal or leaves the Church because of sexual immorality; every time a supposed Christian businessman cheats on an income tax return; anytime hypocrisy lifts its repulsive head—we witness a huge deficiency in integrity.

Abram made a promise to God and then kept it. He didn't allow temptation to get to him. That's integrity.

Fifth Glimmering Quality: Humility

Shortly after the king of Sodom rushed out to meet Abram, a second man also came out for a meeting, a mysterious fellow named Melchizedek. The Bible calls him "priest of God Most High" and says that he told Abram, *"Blessed be Abram of God Most High, Possessor of heaven and earth; and blessed be God Most High, who has delivered your enemies into your hand"* (Genesis 14:18-20). Abram responded to these words by giving Melchizedek 10 percent of everything he had.

Why did Abram do this? And who was this Melchizedek?

Melchizedek is one of the most mystifying figures in all of Scripture. Opinions vary on his historical identity. Some think he was Shem, the son of Noah, who lived a long time (and according to some, still lives today). Some believe he was a monotheistic Gentile king who emerged out of nowhere. Others believe he was Jesus Christ in a pre-incarnate form.

The name Melchizedek means "king of righteousness" and he came from a city called Salem, later known as Jerusalem. As a priest he met Abram with two very familiar elements, bread and wine. And he was the only man Abram recognized as his superior, because after receiving a blessing from Melchizedek, Abram paid him a tithe. The ancients considered tithing an act of submission and worship.

So just as Abram refused to take money from Bera, to keep anyone from thinking that the king of Sodom had made Abram rich, Abram did give money to Melchizedek, to acknowledge God's help and to thank the Lord for giving him victory. Through this act of worship, Abram said, "That's right, God gave us the victory. He is the hero of this story."

This is genuine humility. Abram did not say, "What a strategist I am! With only 318 servants and three friends, we beat four kings." Instead, he took no credit. He made a vow to God that the Lord would get all the glory, and in fulfillment of that vow gave a tithe of all that he possessed. He publicly thanked God for the victory.

No matter how gifted, talented, or successful you are in ministry or in business or anything else, you had better thank God for the success He's given you. You may have great talent—but never think that God is lucky to have you. Paul asks, *What do you have that you did not receive?* (1 Corinthians 4:7). We know that God chooses the foolish things of this world to confound the wise. I'm reminded of that every time somebody says to me, "Oh, Skip, God has used you so magnificently." That only means that I must be right on top of the list of foolish things.

Abram gave all the glory to God for the victory the Lord had given him. In humility he recognized his dependence on God. He acknowledged His grace and mercy in allowing Abram to recover his nephew, Lot. Humility loves to honor God and loathes self-congratulation.

Messy, but Worth It

If you want to make a positive mark on your world, then do everything you can to strengthen your sympathy, bravery, capability, integrity, and humility. Every one of those qualities brings a special power to deal effectively with personal crises. If you want friends who possess those qualities, then strive to be a friend who has those qualities.

That's a nice sentiment, Skip, you might think. *But why should I get involved in the lives of others? That's so messy. I don't want to get involved with their problems; I have enough of my own. I don't even think it's my place. Anyway, what good can one person do? I mean, if I don't do it, so what?*

The truth is, you don't have to get involved. You don't have to care enough to take action. You probably do have enough problems of your own, and few people will blame you if you remain on the sidelines. You don't have to follow Abram's example if you don't want to.

Of course, when you take the self-centered route, you shouldn't expect anyone else to come to your aid in your own time of crisis. You shouldn't expect Jesus to say to you one day, "When I was in prison, you came to visit me." You shouldn't expect anyone to think of you as a person of integrity or bravery or compassion. God will not get much (if any) glory from your life, and people won't feel much (if any) gratitude for your presence.

Abram wasn't like that. When the crisis came, he acted. God used him to bring joy to captives, and Abram thanked God for the privilege of being used.

Look around: there's always a crisis somewhere. As the pastor of a large church, I hear of probably ten or twenty of them every week. I don't mind; I figure that God has called me to help people in crisis however I can.

Things aren't so different in your world. There's always a crisis in somebody's life and trouble in somebody's community. God calls you to get involved, to allow your sympathy to move you to brave, capable, humble action.

And the best thing of all is these are some of the greatest opportunities in life to give glory to God—for everyone to see His goodness and mercy. That's what I mean by the glimmer of the godly in the cauldron of crisis.

MEDITATING ON YOUR MARK

In this chapter we learned the five glimmering qualities that people of faith demonstrate during a time of crisis. In the midst of adverse occasions, Christians should strive to show sympathy, bravery, capability, integrity, and humility.

Sympathy. What concerns you about the state of the world today? How can you move and act on your feelings as an apostle of Christ?

Bravery. Francis Schaeffer said, "I am not a pacifist because pacifism in a fallen world means we must desert the very people that deserve our greatest help." What immediate impressions does this statement bring you?

Capability. Think on the following characteristics: teamwork, strategy, and persistence. How do these traits manifest themselves in your own life?

Integrity. How often do you examine the motives behind your actions? Why do you do what you do?

Humility. In the ancient world, tithing was considered an act of submission and worship. Are you faithful in your own tithing?

MODELING THE MASTER'S MARK

Sympathy. Hebrews 13:3: *"Remember the prisoners as if chained with them—those who are mistreated—since you yourselves are in the body also."*

Bravery. Proverbs 28:1: *"The wicked flee when no one pursues, but the righteous are bold as a lion."*

Capability. Mark 6:7: *"And He called the twelve to Himself, and began to send them out two by two . . ."*

Integrity. Matthew 6:5: *"And when you pray, you shall not be like the hypocrites. For they love to pray standing in the synagogues and on the corners of the streets, that they may be seen by men. Assuredly, I say to you, they have their reward."*

Humility. Deuteronomy 16:17: *"Every man shall give as he is able, according to the blessing of the LORD your God which He has given you."*

MAKING YOUR MARK

Jesus Christ said, *"Assuredly, I say to you, inasmuch as you did it to one of the least of these My brethren, you did it to Me"* (Matthew 25:40). Today, who can you help in a very direct way? Whose burden can you lessen?

CHAPTER SIX

The Journey From Fear to Faith

Despite her fear of heights, a young woman named Jessica decided to learn how to rock climb. She joined a group of experienced climbers who promised to teach her the ropes, quite literally. One day, with the lead climber far above her, Jessica started her slow ascent. When she reached a little rock ledge, she decided to stop and take a break.

When she did, the person above her accidentally snapped a rope. The falling rope hit Jessica's eye and popped out her contact lens. Do you know how difficult it can be to find a contact lens even under normal circumstances? I know, because I lose contact lenses all the time. But to find a lens while rock climbing? It's impossible.

So Jessica found herself, miles from home and with blurred vision, hoping that maybe it had gotten lodged in her eye or somewhere on her clothing. When she arrived at the top of the mountain, she asked her buddies to look in her eye and on her clothing, but they couldn't find the lens anywhere.

As Jessica gazed over the vast mountain landscape, a verse came to her: *"The eyes of the LORD run to and fro throughout the whole earth"* (2 Chronicles 16:9). And so she prayed: "Lord, you see every mountain, every rock, and every leaf under every rock. You know where my contact lens is. Could you let me find it?"

Eventually the time came for Jessica's group to climb down. At the bottom of their descent, they met another group of climbers on their way up. One of those climbers shouted out to Jessica's group, "Hey, did any of you lose a contact lens?"

Amazing, huh? But how he found the lens was even more amazing. He told Jessica he had discovered the lens as he looked down and saw a little ant crawling across the surface of a rock, carrying the lost contact lens on its back.

A lot of people hear this story and say, "What a coincidence." However, Christians call that nothing short of Providence. We recognize a caring God intent on building up the faith of a fearful young woman.

When Jessica's dad, a cartoonist, later heard the story, he drew a picture to illustrate the experience from a unique perspective. He depicted an ant struggling with a contact lens on its back and saying, "Lord, I don't know why you want me to carry this thing. I can't eat it and it's awfully heavy. But if this is what you want me to do, I'll carry it for you."[1]

Genesis tells the story of another journey—not of an ant or of a rock climber, but of Abram. He journeys from the crippling emotion of fear to the strong platform of faith. As he learns what it means to trust God, he grows in his faith. And he shows us a key element of how to make our mark on the world around us.

A Crucial Passage

Genesis 15:1-6 is crucial to understanding the rest of the Bible. Why? Because the last verse of that passage provides the prima facie evidence for how an unrighteous, unholy, sinful person can be made righteous before a holy God. The New Testament quotes it no less than four times to illustrate righteousness by grace alone through faith alone.

After these things the word of the LORD came to Abram in a vision, saying, "Do not be afraid, Abram. I am your shield, your exceedingly great reward." But Abram said, "Lord GOD, what will You give me, seeing I go childless, and the heir of my house is Eliezer of Damascus?" Then Abram said, "Look, You have given me no offspring; indeed one born in my house is my heir!" And behold, the word of the LORD came to him, saying, "This one shall not be your heir, but one who will come from your own body shall be your heir." Then He brought him outside and said, "Look now toward heaven, and count the stars if you are able to number them." And He said to him, "So shall your descendants be." And he believed in the LORD, and He accounted it to him for righteousness.

The world has only two religions, really. One is the religion of human achievement; the other is the religion of divine accomplishment. A huge gulf separates the two. The first says, "I'm going to work my way to God." The second says, "I can't do it, Lord. I need you to do it for me." One is all by human effort; the other is all by divine grace. One is earned, and the other is a gift.

Most of the men and women we meet depend on the first religion, don't they? They stake their eternal future, their whole life journey, on their achievements. They think if they're just good enough—if they think good thoughts and go to church and do this good deed and help that needy person—they'll make it to Heaven.

Not Abram. He believed God, and the Lord counted his faith as righteousness.

But how did this Gentile—with no Law of Moses, as yet no covenant of circumcision, and no older believers to show him the right path—somehow learn the only way to become righteous before God? That question prompts a second one, this one aimed at us: How do we become righteous before a holy God?

We find sound answers to both questions as we retrace the four stages of Abram's journey.

Stage One: The Fear of Man

Abram's journey of faith began in fear. Genesis 15:1 says: *"After these things the word of the LORD came to Abram in a vision, saying, 'Do not be afraid, Abram. I am your shield, your exceedingly great reward.'"*

This is the first appearance in the Bible of the phrase "do not be afraid." It pops up another sixty-two times, but here its use indicates something troubled Abram deeply. God doesn't just walk up to somebody who's unafraid and say, "Don't be afraid." Apparently, fear gripped Abram's heart. What made him afraid? I can think of a few possibilities.

First, Abram might simply have suffered from post-battle blues. Military history recounts many stories of veterans who acted with courage and bravery during a battle, but who afterward felt their emotions catching up with them. Today we call it post-traumatic stress disorder. They fought their battles with courage, but later on had flashbacks or nighttime visions in which they relived the whole scene. Abram might have suffered from post-traumatic stress.

Second, the vision itself might have frightened Abram. In the Bible, visions from God often scared those who had them. When Isaac had a vision from God, the first thing God said to him was, "Don't be afraid." The same thing happened to Jacob. The angel who came to Mary, bearing the news that she would give birth to Jesus, said to her,

"Don't be afraid." A later angelic visit to Joseph, Mary's betrothed husband, began with, "Don't be afraid."

When an angel brought Daniel a vision, the prophet described his reaction: *"No strength remained in me; for my vigor was turned to frailty in me, and I retained no strength. ... Then he said to me, 'Do not fear, Daniel....'"* (Daniel 10:8, 12). After an earlier vision, he said, *"I, Daniel, fainted and was sick for days"* (8:27). Obviously, the apparitions were scary. Even the Apostle John, who saw Jesus as described in Revelation, said, *"I fell at His feet as dead"* (1:17). The problem with this explanation is that Abram responds with fear only this one time. God appeared to him at other times in a vision.

What frightened Abram? I believe it was the fear of man. Notice that the chapter begins, "After these things." So after his battle with the four kings, Abram had this vision. Perhaps he thought, *Now what do I do? If I remember right, Chedorlaomer laid waste to five cities and their armies; I'm just one man with three hundred and eighteen servants-turned-soldiers. Yes, we got everything back—but what happens if they retaliate? I'm toast.* This thought may well have kept Abram awake at night. The fear of man may have made Abram tremble—and so God said to him, "Do not be afraid, Abram. I am your shield, your exceedingly great reward."

In addition, something else happened "after these things." Abram met the king of Sodom, Bera, who offered him a reward—and Abram turned it down flat. Taking a reward wasn't like an honorarium for services rendered; it meant forming an alliance for the future in case of impending attack. So by refusing the reward, Abram cut off all dependence on man—but now he might have reconsidered his decision.

And so God came to him and said, "Abram, I am your shield, so do not be afraid."

You may be walking in Abram's sandals. You feel afraid. A coworker, a neighbor, a relative, or somebody else has risen against you. Maybe you're facing a lawsuit. Maybe you've heard about coming layoffs. Maybe somebody has threatened you. Whatever your circumstances, you feel afraid. You know what the Bible says—*"The fear of man brings a snare, but whoever trusts in the LORD shall be safe"* (Proverbs 29:25)—but still you tremble.

Did you know that fear is one of the most destructive of human emotions? It debilitates and freezes and paralyzes anyone in its grip. We often have irrational fears, and we might even recognize them as such—but whenever we give in to them, they keep us from moving ahead.

A study at the University of Wisconsin reported, "Forty percent of our fears are unfounded; they're worries about things that will never happen."[2] We all know what it's like to have irrational fear. It happens with kids, with teenagers, with young adults, and with older adults. Have you ever read Shel Silverstein's children's poem *"What If…"*? It says:

Last night while I lay thinking here,
some what-ifs crawled inside my ear,
and pranced and partied all night long,
and sang their same old what-if song.
What if they've closed the swimming pool?
What if I'm dumb in school?
What if I get beat up?
What if there's poison in my cup?
What if I start to cry?
What if I just get sick and die?
What if I flunk the test?
What if green hair grows on my chest?[3]

Kids have irrational fears—but so do adults. Even Christian adults have them. Abram certainly did.

When you find yourself afraid, you need exactly what Abram needed: a shield called God. The problem with the other shields people use is that they're other people or the government or fill-in-the-blank—and all of them can let you down. And when you get let down, you feel more fearful than ever. So God told Abram, "Do not be afraid, Abram. I am your shield."

Stage Two: Fading Hope

Abram no doubt was delighted to hear that God would be his shield—but even such wonderful news didn't take away all of his worries. *"LORD God,"* Abram replied, *"what will You give me, seeing I go childless, and the heir of my house is Eliezer of Damascus?"* (Genesis 15:2).

Notice the route of this man's journey. Abram began in fear; God answered his fear with a promise. Then Abram responded with a rebuttal. "But," Abram said, "what are you going to give me?" The rebuttal reveals Abram's fading hope in the prior promise of God.

The *New Living Translation* renders this verse, *"O Sovereign LORD, what good are all your blessings when I don't even have a son?"* You can hear the deep emotion in Abram's words. Several times God has made promises to Abram. In Genesis 12, God promised Abram that He would make him into a great nation; but you've got to have children for that promise to come true, and Abram didn't have any. Later in the same chapter, God promised Abram that He would give the Land of Promise to his descendants; but how do you have descendants when you don't even have any children? And in the very next chapter God promised (more than once) that Abram would have more descendants than the dust of the Earth—but again, where were his kids?

Abram didn't object to the promises; he considered them all wonderful. He had only one problem: no kids. By now, Abram was getting really old. The clock was ticking, he was getting elderly, and his wife was no spring chicken, either.

When Abram left Haran, he was seventy-five years old. The events in Genesis 15 probably happened ten years later. God had yet to fulfill His promise—Abram had simply grown older. Ten years is a long time to wait when God says, "You're going to have a lot of kids and their descendants are going to own all this land."

"That's great, Lord," Abram essentially said. "Those are great promises and I appreciate them all. I really do. It's just that I don't have any kids yet. All I have is this servant named Eliezer and he's going to inherit it all."

Who was Eliezer of Damascus? Some think that he was a servant whom Abram had adopted. But Damascus was the financial metropolis of that area and a lot of scholars believe that Eliezer was not only a guy who hung around with Abram, but that the name identified a financial institution, the title of a banking house. So to say, "Eliezer of Damascus," was like saying, "Bank of the West." If that's true, we can appreciate Abram's fading hope. "Lord, those are cool promises, but I don't have any kids—and what good is all of the wealth and all of the land if, when I die, it's all going to the bank, anyway?" That was his fear.

And Abram was honest with God. He was not defiant; he was not shaking his fist; he was just truthful: "God, help me to understand. I'm learning here. I don't get how this is all going to work. I guess you mean that Eliezer is going to inherit it all—is that what you mean?"

How do you respond when you see your hope fading? What do you do when the promises of God appear to be losing their luster? How do you react when the thing you've most anticipated appears nowhere in sight? If you're like a lot of people, you do everything but what you should do first—talk to God. You talk to the bank, to your family, to your buddies, to your neighbors, but not to God. And all the while God is saying, "Psst! Hey, over here. Talk to Me!"

"Thanks, God, but I don't need to talk to you. It's not that bad yet." Too many of us view prayer like those little red boxes in buildings: "For Emergency Use Only."

Abram immediately talked to God about his problem. He prayed about it.

When you make prayer your first route, then it won't have to become your last resort. Jesus told His disciples, *"Men ought always to pray, and not to faint"* (Luke 18:1, KJV). Why do so many of us adopt the philosophy, "I'd rather faint first"?

In Genesis 15, Abram teaches us much about prayer and about how to leave our mark on the world. First, he's honest with God. He doesn't try to flatter Him or use words he doesn't mean. He honored Him and blessed Him and praised Him, but he didn't try to impress God with his language. God's been around a long time and He's heard every prayer from the beginning of time. I think He can handle your honesty. C. H. Spurgeon once said, "There is no secret of my heart that I would not pour into His ear."

Second, Abram is very specific. In two verses he spells out his concern, and then spells it out again in the next verse. He tells God exactly what's going on; he describes his entire predicament. God doesn't need the information, of course; it's not as though He's up in Heaven saying, "Oh, that's interesting, Abe. I didn't know that. What else?" The point, for both Abram and us, is that the more specific our prayers, the more specific the results. Would you walk into a restaurant and say, "I have a food need in general, so please bring me something"? No, you very specifically order from the menu.

To make our mark on the world, we should follow Abram's example and be very honest and very specific in our prayers.

Stage Three: Faithful Promises

Abram began his journey in the fear of man, so God came to him and answered his fear with a promise: "I'm your shield, your great reward." Then Abram responded to God's promise with a rebuttal: "Yeah, but I don't have any kids." So now God answers his rebuttal—with what? With an explanation? No. He answers with another promise.

Why do so many of us think that God owes us an explanation for what He's doing or not doing? As if that would help. Can I tell you something? You don't live off explanations; you live off promises.

My son fell off a wall years ago and cut his tongue with his upper teeth, so deeply that you could see all the way through the flesh. He almost bit his tongue in two. So I took him to the hospital. The doctor didn't give us a bunch of explanations about what had happened. He didn't say, "The anterior dorsal part of the tongue has been incised by the upper teeth, which caused trauma to the lingual nerve; and that's why there is this persistent parasthesia, or tingling, in the tongue." We couldn't have cared less. Do you know what he said to us? "Stitches will be out in two weeks. Your boy will be fine. He'll be able to taste normally and will be able to feel again." I could live with that.

Notice that God repeated to Abram the same promise He had given him before; He didn't give him anything really new. "You're going to have descendants, Abram, and a lot of them."

Do you know what I love about God? He often condescends to our low level of belief. Abram had heard this promise already, but God didn't say, "You idiot! Are you deaf? I'm not going to tell you again what I already said—go back and read it in the previous chapter." No, God repeated the same promise.

Has God ever stooped to repeating something to you? You knew the truth, you'd read the verse, but the way you lived suggested that you had forgotten it.

In college I found myself running out of money and living off of peanut butter and jelly sandwiches. When the jelly ran out, it was peanut butter sandwiches without the jelly. When the bread ran out, it was just peanut butter on a spoon. I'd been reading my Bible and knew that I'd get paid eventually; but it got really tight and I knew it could be a week without anything but peanut butter. I read the promises of God, but I didn't get too excited about them. "Yeah, okay, cool." But I kept wringing my hands.

One day an IRS check came in with my tax refund. I opened it and jumped for joy. "They're going to pay me this much? This is great!"

Immediately, I felt the Holy Spirit tapping at my heart: "How do you know the government is good for it?"

"I've got a check—they promised."

"But I've been promising you all week long that I'd provide, and you didn't seem all that excited. Now you're excited because I answered your prayer using their check?"

Oh.

But the Lord stooped to my level and repeated the same promise.

Notice something else in Abram's journey: God not only repeated the promise; He also clarified it. He said, "No, Abram, Eliezer won't be your heir. This is how it's going to work: When I say you're going to have a son, I don't mean you're going to adopt anybody, or that the money's going to the bank and this guy will become your heir. A son is going to come from your own body, buddy."

And God didn't stop there. He then expanded on the promise. "Look at the stars," He instructed Abram. Moments before, God had told Abram to look down at the dust: "Just as you can't count the dust, you won't be able to count the multitudes of your descendants." When Abram finished looking down, God told him, "Now look up, at the stars. Can you count them? I didn't think so. So shall your descendants be." God takes the same promise, then clarifies it, and expands it by having Abram compare the number of his future descendants to the limitless, starry host.

The next time you find yourself in a jam, begin to falter, and think, *It's too late, God has gone way past the deadline; He should have acted by now* ... go outside at night. Get out of the city where you can escape the light pollution and look up. Let the stars dance for you. They shout out the promises of God.

How big is your God? When you get in a jam that really worries you, does your God tend to shrink? Get a bigger view of Him. The Bible says, *"Who has measured the waters in the hollow of His hand?..."* (Isaiah 40:12).

Last night I needed a bigger vision of God, so I took a little walk, looked up, and tried to calculate my location in the universe. The Milky Way is 10,000 light years by 100,000 light years long. If I could travel at the speed of light, I could circle the Earth seven-and-a-half times in one second. I'd zip past the moon in one-and-a-half seconds; past Venus in two minutes and eighteen seconds; past Mercury in four-and-a-half minutes; and past the sun in seven-and-a-half minutes. But I'd have to travel for 100,000 years to make it from the front yard to the backyard of the Milky Way galaxy. And after 100,000 years, I'd just be getting started in my trip through the universe—because billions of other galaxies lie beyond.

When I look up and make these calculations, I realize just how little I am and just how big God is. And yet He invites me to dump all my problems on Him. So I start thinking of His promises in a new way. "Yeah," I say, "He's trustworthy. He can handle this."

Stage Four: Faith in God

Abram traveled a long way on his journey from fear to faith. The Bible records his fourth step: *"And he believed in the* LORD, *and He accounted it to him for righteousness"* (Genesis 15:6). In this verse, the word "believe" is the Hebrew term *amain*, or "amen."

"Abe," God said, "look at those stars—that's how many kids you're going to have when I'm finished making you into a nation."

And Abram replied, "Amen! Right on! So be it."

The word "amen" (or believe) means far more than an intellectual acknowledgment. It's not as though Abram said, "Yeah, right. Whatever." In this context, the word means, "to lean on." In Hebrew it means, "to nourish, nurse, or support." The idea is that God said it, and Abram leaned fully on what He said. He was nourished with that promise—and that's faith. Abram leaned on God's promise. And how did God respond? The Lord counted Abram's faith as righteousness.

In other words, that little act of faith—believing God's promise—was enough to make Abram right before God. The Bible doesn't say, "Abram believed God, and God said, 'Great, Abram! Now you do these thirty-six things, get baptized, join a church, keep the Law, and then we'll see.'" No. He said, "You're righteous, Abram. You are right before me because you've trusted me. You've believed that

I will fulfill my promise, even though you haven't seen it happen yet."

The Hinge of Scripture

Four key passages in the New Testament—Romans 4, Galatians 3, Hebrews 11, and James 2—all refer to Abram's trust in the promise of God. I'd say that the whole of Scripture depends on the "hinge paragraph" of Genesis 15:1-6. That's how important it is. This tells us not only how Abram came to be counted righteous before God, but also how we can gain the same status.

Paul declared that Abraham was justified through his faith in God's promise—not by his works. And the apostle takes special care to point out that God accounted Abraham righteous before he received the rite of circumcision, *"... that he might be the father of all those who believe, though they are uncircumcised, that righteousness might be imputed to them also"* (Romans 4:11).

Many people think they get to Heaven like the frog who worked his way out of a bucket of milk. The frog couldn't merely jump out because of the bucket's tall sides, so he just kept paddling and paddling until he churned some butter. And when that butter firmed up, it gave him a launching pad from which he could jump to his freedom. The moral of the story, they say, is to try hard and keep paddling; that's how to get to Heaven.

Both Abram and Paul would say, "No way!" In fact, there's only one way to get right before God, and that is by faith in His promise. Not by circumcision, not by baptism, not by joining a church, not by the Law. But by faith alone.

Paul wrote that Abram *"believed God, and it was accounted to him for righteousness"* (Galatians 3:6). The Greek term *elogisthe* is translated "accounted." It's a banking term that means, "to apply something to one's credit."

Picture a ledger with two sides, a debit side and a credit side. When he arrives from Paganville, Abram is spiritually bankrupt before God. When God calls him for His own purposes, Abram has no way to earn his righteousness before God. So the debit side of Abram's ledger is packed. At the same time, he has nothing on his credit side. Yet the moment he says, "I believe you, God. Amen," God changes the books and writes on the credit side of Abram's ledger, "Righteous before God."

It's the same with us. Our debit side overflows with the debt of our sins. The credit side remains empty, despite our good works, religion, church attendance, baptism, rituals, or anything else. We know this. All have sinned and fallen short of the glory of God. The wages of sin is death. Without the shedding of blood, there is no remission of sins. Somebody had to die for our sins, and God ordained that Jesus Christ die for us, in our place. So it's as if God totaled up the number of sins that you and I and everyone else would ever commit, and then calculated that the shed blood of His Son provided adequate payment for them all. If you believe in Jesus' work—not in your works, but in His finished work—then God counts you as righteous.

Sometimes people try telling me about all they gave up to follow Christ. Oh, please! What did anybody ever give up to follow Jesus? Meaninglessness? Hell? Yeah, you've really sacrificed a lot. It reminds me of the man who suddenly received a huge inheritance, complete with a new mansion, a colossal bank account, a fleet of Mercedes—and he bragged that to get it, he had to give up his broken-down van, abandoned by a stagnant pond in a desolate part of town.

Horatio Spafford wrote the famous song, "It Is Well With My Soul," after he lost his four daughters in a tragedy at sea. Too often we forget the third verse:

My sin, oh, the bliss of this glorious thought!
My sin, not in part but the whole,
Is nailed to the cross, and I bear it no more.
Praise the Lord, praise the Lord, O my soul!

When you say, "I am saved by the finished work of Jesus Christ. I trust Him, I love Him, I believe Him," then God says, "You're in. You're my child. I'll receive you. I will justify you, I will declare you righteous." None of us act in righteous ways all the time, but nevertheless, He declared us righteous when we placed our faith in His Son.

That's His decision, and I'm glad He made it!

MEDITATING ON THE MARK

In this chapter we learned how Abram's belief and faith in the Lord was accounted to him for righteousness. The journey to becoming righteous before our holy God has four stages: the fear of man, fading hope, faithful promises, and faith in God.

Fear. Abram was afraid of man and of his potential responses. How can you remind yourself that your shield against coworkers, relatives, and others is God himself?

Fading. What begins with fear in Abram is followed by a promise from God. Yet Abram responded to God with a rebuttal of fading hope. When has one of God's promises been met by disbelief or despair on your part?

Faithful. God doesn't answer Abram with an explanation, but with another promise. How does God's incredible faithfulness demonstrate itself in your everyday life?

Faith. Because Abram leaned fully on the promise of God, it was accounted to him for righteousness. What do you do personally when your hope is fading? Do you truly trust in the promises of God?

MODELING THE MASTER'S MARK

Fear. Psalm 27:1: *"The LORD is my light and my salvation; whom shall I fear? The LORD is the strength of my life; of whom shall I be afraid?"*

Fading. Mark 9:24: *"Immediately the father of the child cried out and said with tears, 'Lord, I believe; help my unbelief!'"*

Faithful. Lamentations 3:22-23: *"Through the LORD's mercies we are not consumed, because His compassions fail not. They are new every morning; great is Your faithfulness."*

Faith. Proverbs 3:5-6: *"Trust in the LORD with all your heart, and lean not on your own understanding; in all your ways acknowledge Him, and He shall direct your paths."*

MAKING YOUR MARK

Read Romans 4:1-4. Commit to memory Romans 4:3. Step out in faith and do something wonderful for God this week: serve at a homeless shelter, help an elderly person with their shopping, or volunteer in your local children's library.

CHAPTER SEVEN

Taking the Long Way Around

I travel a lot. Once when I took a trip to Singapore from Los Angeles, I asked the flight attendant, "How long is this leg of the journey?"

"Nineteen hours and twenty minutes," she replied. Since I had to fly from Albuquerque first, that meant it took a whole day to get there and another whole day to get back.

On another trip to the Middle East, I returned home with Franklin Graham from Jordan through Germany. We were supposed to take an early flight out of Germany, but our plane stopped in Austria to let passengers out. Franklin said to me, "You know, you ought to get out right here and rent a car and drive to Germany. It's only a couple of hours, and there's some beautiful scenery."

Okay, I thought, and then said, "Hey, you ought to come with me."

"Noi!" he replied. That's Franklin's way of saying, "Okay."

So we got off the airplane, rented a car, and drove away, thinking we'd arrive in Germany in a couple of hours.

After nine hours on the Autobahn—taking full advantage of its no speed limit—we arrived at our hotel at 2 A.M. I looked at Franklin as if to say, *Are you nuts? This thing took much longer than we anticipated.*

I know some people who prefer driving to flying. I know a businessman who crisscrosses America by car. He will not fly. And it's not economy; it's fear. He thinks it's safer to drive, even though plenty of studies insist it's seven times safer to fly than to drive. But flying scares some people, just like it scares some people to wholeheartedly trust in God. They can't see Him; they don't hear His audible voice, so to trust in Him seems scary. It's much safer to trust their own judgment, they think.

But the best and safest way to travel through life is to follow God's path. Any other travel plans will put you on a long and painful detour. I remember the late Vance Havner saying, "The detour is always worse than the main road."

Abram and Sarai made this painful discovery for themselves when they chose to circumvent the direct will of God. As we read about their misadventure in Genesis 16, tuck two additional verses in your mind. One says, *"He who trusts in his own heart is a fool"* (Proverbs 28:26). And the second says, *"But those who wait on the LORD shall renew their strength; they shall mount up with wings like eagles, they shall run and not be weary, they shall walk and not faint"* (Isaiah 40:31).

As we watch Abram and Sarai's unfortunate journey, we can measure their progress by identifying four important mile markers along the way. And we will see that to leave a positive mark on the world, it's always best to stick to the main road—God's will.

Mile Marker One: Vulnerability

It had been eleven years since God first said to Abram, "You're going to have a son and lots of descendants. I'm going to make you into a great nation." I bet from the moment God made His promise, every time Sarai had a twinge of a pain or walked in an odd sort of way, Abram perked up and said, "What could this mean? Are you pregnant?"

I'm sure the routine got old after eleven years, especially when you're a seventy-five-year-old woman. It had to feel more than a little embarrassing. In fact, Sarai might have thought, *Waiting for this pregnancy is either faith or senility; I don't know which.*

And yet they both waited. And waited. And waited.

Waiting demonstrates our vulnerability as almost nothing else can.

We may not admit it, but waiting on God and His timing is one of the hardest things we will ever do. No one likes to wait. Don't you hate it when you make a phone call and you get a recording that says, "Your call is very important to us, please hold"? We hate lines—on the freeway or at Disneyland or at the DMV. Nobody likes to wait.

I knew a doctor many years ago who played a cruel joke on patients in the San Bernardino Hospital. One day, as a very tired resident, he walked into the emergency waiting room. The seats were filled with people, all waiting for someone to call their name.

"Anybody here waiting to see a doctor?" he asked.

Twenty-five hands immediately went up.

"Well, you've seen one," he said, and turned around and walked away.

I suppose a lot of people think God is like that doctor. "Oh, He's there; He's just not doing anything. He's not moving when I want Him to move."

Some of us nod our heads vigorously when we read Isaiah's observation about God: *"Truly You are God, who hides Yourself"* (Isaiah 45:15).

Where is God? Where has He been? When we wait on God, we often get impatient. We want to push a little harder, to speed things up. We all know by experience the truth pointed out by Solomon: *"Hope deferred makes the heart sick"* (Proverbs 13:12). So we think, *Well then, I'll make things happen. I have a free will. I have two good arms, two good legs, and a good mind. I'm going to push things along a bit.*

But in doing so we forget Isaiah's clear counsel: *"Those who wait on the LORD shall renew their strength"* (Isaiah 40:31).

Theologically, we know that God has a perfect timetable. We know He does everything right on time—not too soon, and never too late. But we wonder why God sometimes waits so long to act on our behalf. Why do the hours turn into days, the days into weeks, the weeks into months, the months into years? Abram and Sarai surely had the same question as they pondered why God waited so long to give them the son He had promised.

Why does God wait so long? And why did He make Abram and Sarai wait so long?

We find some insight from the Book of Hebrews: *"Therefore from one man, and him as good as dead, were born as many as the stars of the sky in multitude—innumerable as the sand which is by the seashore"* (11:12). Isn't that a great way to describe an old guy? Especially a venerated patriarch? "As good as dead."

Do you know why God waited so long to fulfill His promise to Abram? God wanted Abram as good as dead, physically. He wanted to fulfill His promise in such a way that no one could doubt that He was the One who made it all happen. He wanted to make His work so obvious that everyone would say, "That's miraculous! Old guys and gals like Abram and Sarai don't have kids; that must be God." And in that way, God got all the glory.

If you are waiting on God for something, consider that He may have you waiting for the same reason He put Abram and Sarai in the waiting room. God wants to get all the glory in your life, and perhaps the best way to do that is by fulfilling His promise in such a way that everybody will know that He's the One who made it happen.

Someone once wrote, "You can make the clock strike before the hour by putting your hand on it, but it will strike wrong. You can tear the rosebud open before its time, but you will mar its beauty. You may spoil many gifts of blessing that God is preparing for you because of your own eager haste."[1]

The first mile marker on this long detour taken by Abram and Sarai—vulnerability, waiting on God—took its toll. And if we don't learn from their mistakes, it will take its toll on us, too.

Mile Marker Two: Impetuosity

The Lord doesn't need our help in working out His plans, but when we feel as though we've waited too long for Him to act, sometimes we think our ideas might work better than His. So we act impetuously—we plot for God. That's the detour Abram and Sarai chose to take.

Now we have every reason to believe that Abram and Sarai acted as they did from the highest of intentions. I suppose that one night, over a candlelight dinner in their tent, they had a little conversation. As they talked about their childlessness, Sarai may have said, "You know, Abe, I understand that you really want me to have this kid. But come on; look at me! I'm seventy-five and I've always been infertile. Exactly what did God tell you all those times He appeared to you?"

"Well," Abram might have said, "He told me that we're going to have kids. In fact, God said a son would come from my own body."

"Ah, exactly, Abe! He said he'd come from your body; he said nothing about it coming from my body. So take Hagar, my Egyptian maidservant. She's young and maybe through her God will fulfill His promise to have the child come from your body."

Let's understand that in the ancient world, this practice of surrogate mothering was common practice. The Canaanites did it all the time. So when Sarai suggested this plan, it wouldn't have struck Abram as odd or unseemly. But I do think the two of them made three major mistakes.

First, they took matters into their own hands. Paul could have asked them, as he did the churches centuries later, *"Having begun in the Spirit, are you now being made perfect by the flesh?"* (Galatians 3:3). At the beginning, Abram and Sarai believed God and were content to wait. But that time had come to an end. Now they decided to turn to the flesh for help.

Have you ever waited so long that you started wondering if God went on vacation? Or perhaps that His plan could stand some improvement? And so you resorted to impetuosity. Maybe you've even found yourself counseling God: "Lord, come into my office, let's talk. We've waited on you long enough. Now, I've been to college, God. I've got a plan, and if you follow my plan, it'll work."

But as I've said, God doesn't need our help. Taking matters into our own hands only leads to very bad and very long detours. Proverbs 3:5-6 says, *"Trust in the LORD with all your heart, and lean not on your own understanding; in all your ways acknowledge Him, and He shall direct your paths."* A Jewish proverb says, "It's better to ask the way ten times than to take the wrong road once."

We see nothing in Genesis 16 about Abram stopping and saying, "Okay, you've got a point there, Sarai. But let's build another altar. We've done that in the past and it's always worked for us. Let's pray about it. Let's talk to God, and then we'll wait for a while." But nothing like that ever took place.

I read about a guide from Arabia who frequently traversed the deserts. Somehow, he never got lost. His secret? He always carried a homing pigeon, so no matter where he ended up, if he didn't know which direction to go, he'd throw the bird in the air. One of its legs was attached to a fine cord, and, of course, the homing pigeon always flew in the direction of home. So the guide always knew in what direction he needed to go.

So while you're waiting—maybe getting impetuous, frustrated, and angry—do you throw the pigeon up once in a while? Get your bearings. Ask for directions. Wait on the Lord in prayer, because every time you and I try to do the work of the Lord in the energy of our own flesh, we'll end up taking a sad and unfortunate detour. Guaranteed.

Now, don't misunderstand. I'm not recommending that we should be passive, lazy, or uninvolved. But as we move forward, we need to depend on Him. We should never move independently of Him. Bottom line? Don't take the matter into your own hands.

Abram and Sarai made their second major mistake when they pursued a personal goal instead of the glory of God. Sarai told Abram, *"The LORD has restrained me from bearing children"* (Genesis 16:2). Can you hear a hint of disappointment and even blame in her words?

Have you ever heard Satan whisper anything like this into your ears? "The Lord's holding out on you. If He loved you, why would He withhold that from you?" Or "Why would God want you to stay in this marriage if you're not happy? You know God wants you to be happy." We've all heard that slimy voice.

Sarai's words also revealed her ultimate goal. She wanted Abram to impregnate Hagar: "That I might obtain children by her." That was her primary concern. "We're going to do this because I have a goal, Abe. My goal is to have a child."

But God didn't want Sarai merely to have a child. God wanted her to have a certain child, in a certain way, who came from both Abram and Sarai. Why? So God would get the glory.

Jesus taught us to pray, "*Our Father in heaven, hallowed be Your name. Your kingdom come. Your will be done on earth as it is in heaven*" (Matthew 6:9-10). Do you ever filter your prayer requests through God's glory? Here's what you should do: begin to pray for something, but then pause and ask, "If God were to answer this prayer in my way, would He get greater honor? Would His name be more magnified? Would His Kingdom be built up?" God is not some divine bellhop whom you ring up and say, "Room service. Now. I need something; I'm uncomfortable."

Abram and Sarai committed their final big mistake when they allowed themselves to be swayed by their former lifestyle. Sure, the culture around them accepted the practice of surrogate motherhood through a household servant. Archaeologists discovered an ancient engraving in Canaan that said: "If Gallemnu bears children, Shanema shall not take another wife. But if Gallemnu fails to bear children, she shall get for him a slave girl as a concubine. In that case, Gallemnu herself shall have authority over her offspring." Abram and Sarai knew that all their neighbors accepted the practice. So Sarai said to her husband, "Look, everybody's doing this. It isn't a big deal for us to take this gal and have a child through her. Abram, you take her as your second wife, and we'll just call it a promise fulfilled." But God already had made it clear: "You're not of this culture, Abram. I'm calling you to be something different, something special."

A few years later, when Hagar fled from Sarai because of her mistreatment, an angel of the Lord called out to

Hagar and called her "Sarai's maid." (See Genesis 16:8.) By calling Hagar Sarai's maid—and not Abram's wife—the angel revealed that God didn't recognize this marriage.

Our past, our culture, and our former lifestyle have a way of influencing our lives, don't they? We tend to take certain actions because—"Well, everybody does it." But what is socially acceptable is not necessarily divinely acceptable. In fact, usually it's not. Just because something is legal doesn't make it right. Abortion is legal; fornication between consenting adults is legal; homosexuality is legal—but none of these practices are right spiritually. All of them are wrong.

God's people are to not to behave as everyone else. In 1 Samuel we learn that Israel wanted a king so the nation could be like all the other nations around it. But from the beginning, God's whole point was that the Israelites were not to be like other nations; they were to be a distinctive people. Paul later wrote to his fellow Christians: *"And do not be not conformed to this world, but be transformed by the renewing of your mind"* (Romans 12:2). Or as the Phillips translation says: "Don't let the world squeeze you into its mold."

It's hard to make a mark on your world for God when you leave Him out of the equation. And impetuosity can leave you exactly in that predicament.

Mile Marker Three: Legacy

We all leave a legacy; we have no choice. The only choice we have is whether we'll leave a good legacy or a bad one. And when we get impetuous and refuse to wait on God—even when the waiting gets long—chances are we won't leave a legacy for good.

Abram followed Sarai's counsel and conceived a child with Hagar—and that decision totally changed the dynamics of his household. When Hagar saw that she was pregnant, she "despised" Sarai, her infertile mistress. Sarai quickly noticed Hagar's change of attitude; she went to Abram and said:

> *My wrong be upon you! I gave my maid into your embrace; and when she saw that she had conceived, I became despised in her eyes. The LORD judge between you and me.* (Genesis 16:5)

Now Abram had a problem. And how did he respond? He said to his wife, *"Indeed your maid is in your hand; do to her as you please"* (Genesis 16:6). Given this green light, Sarai dealt harshly with Hagar, who ran away into the wilderness. A little while later the angel of the Lord found Hagar sitting near a spring of water, apparently on her way to Egypt. When the angel asked where she had come from and where she was going, she answered, *"I am fleeing from the presence of my mistress Sarai"* (Genesis 16:8).

But the angel instructed: *"Return to your mistress, and submit yourself under her hand"* (Genesis 16:9). Not exactly what she wanted to hear! And then he added:

> *I will multiply your descendants exceedingly, so that they shall not be counted for multitude.... Behold, you are with child, and you shall bear a son. You shall call his name Ishmael, because the LORD has heard your affliction. He shall be a wild man; his hand shall be against every man, and every man's hand against him. And he shall dwell in the presence of all his brethren.* (Genesis 16:10-12)

A Scottish author named George MacDonald once said, "In whatever man does without God, he must fail miserably or succeed more miserably." Abram and Sarai succeeded in their plot more miserably.

But this is such a small infraction in the whole scheme of life, we think. *Surely this isn't going to set them back much. The grace of God covers it all.*

No doubt that God's grace covers all our sins. No question that God forgave Abram and Sarai for their impetuosity—but even today, we continue to suffer from the results of their sin. And they felt the results immediately.

First, they felt interpersonal stress. An angry Sarai vented her frustration, blamed her husband, and mistreated Hagar so badly that the young woman fled into the desert. Victor Hugo was right: "Hell hath no fury like a woman scorned." And when this woman felt scorned, her jealousy raged.

We see the same pattern today. Whenever we stop trusting God, we start blaming others. When we stop trusting God, we fault everyone and everything around us and make life miserable for everybody.

Have you noticed that, throughout this story, Abram seemed so passive? He acted like a wet noodle. He let his wife talk him into marrying an Egyptian servant, and when that didn't work out, he said, "Hey, do whatever you need to do. Hagar is in your hands. You handle it."

God instructs men to be men. We are to be loving and servant-like, even as we remain genuine leaders in our homes. That's the role to which God has called all husbands.

Many years ago James Dobson wrote:

> It's my guess that ninety percent of the divorces that occur every year involve an extremely busy husband who's in love with his work and tends to be somewhat insensitive, unromantic, and non-

communicative, married to a lonely, vulnerable, romantic woman who has severe doubts about her worth as a human being. They become a matched team. He works like a horse and she nags.[1]

He could have been talking about Abram and Sarai. Abram was out there doing his thing, Sarai felt unhappy with it, tried to push her agenda—and it all backfired.

Second, Abram and Sarai's mistake led to an international crisis. Ishmael became the father of the Arabic nations, while Isaac (the son Abram and Sarai would have later) became the father of the Jewish race. This is where the Arab-Israeli conflict started. Right here. The conflict has already raged for four thousand years. You'd think that after such a long time, it would pass. You'd think that four millennia of arguing and dissension and fighting would eventually lead to some kind of peace—for exhaustion's sake, if nothing else.

But it's only getting worse.

Suicide bombers, multiplied deaths in Gaza, threats to exterminate Israel and push its people into the sea, 9/11—do you see the connection? Four thousand years after the births of Abram's two sons, the descendants of Ishmael are still fighting the descendants of Isaac. Talk about longevity of disobedience!

Whatever a man sows, he will reap. You might sow a handful of seeds and get back an acre of crop. Sow to the wind, the prophet said, and you'll reap the whirlwind. (See Hosea 8:7.) Abram and Sarai had no idea of the kind of legacy that would come from their impetuous decision.

But it doesn't end there—we have to consider the final phase of their journey.

Mile Marker Four: Epiphany

Genesis 16 tells the sad story of blundering, sinning, and suffering mankind—but also of an intervening God who is both gracious and merciful. Through God's grace and mercy, Hagar had an epiphany, a sudden realization of the Lord's care for her and goodness to her.

After the Angel of the Lord finished speaking to Hagar, she *"called the name of the LORD who spoke to her, You-Are-the-God-Who-Sees; for she said, 'Have I also here seen Him who sees me?'"* (Genesis 16:13). This is the first mention in Scripture of the Angel of the Lord. Not an angel, but the Angel of the Lord, the messenger above all messengers. Some think the term refers to Gabriel; others disagree because the Angel of the Lord identifies himself as God, and people who see him call him exactly that—both in this passage and in others.

Regardless, the appearance of the Angel of the Lord exemplifies the mercy of God. He pursues Hagar despite her abandonment by Sarai and Abram. Notice that the Angel of the Lord "found" Hagar in the desert. She wasn't looking for God; God was looking for her.

I have discovered that God is more interested in us than we are in Him—even though we think, *Oh no, I'm here to seek God with all my heart.* Maybe. But in a comparative sense, the Bible says: *"There is none who seeks after God"* (Romans 3:11). But God seeks us, looks for us, and takes the initiative with us. He pursued Hagar in spite of her abandonment, and He blessed Abram and Sarai in spite of their disobedience.

And don't think you're left out. God is seeking you, calling you, pursuing you. His grace and mercy seek you out, every bit as much as they did Hagar or Abram and Sarai. That's an epiphany worth having!

Did you notice that the promise God gave to Hagar closely parallels the promise He gave to Abram? He said to her, "I'm going to make your descendants multiply. You're going to have so many of them that you won't be able to count them all."

The Angel of the Lord told Hagar to name the child Ishmael, which means, "God hears" or "God shall hear." So every time Hagar called her son to come in, wash up, or go to bed, she was reminded of the mercy of God in her life. She recalled the intervening, gracious pursuit of God. God hears!

A verse in the New Testament dovetails nicely with this story: *"But where sin abounded, grace abounded much more"* (Romans 5:20). The verse doesn't mean that God winks at sin or that the key to receiving abundant grace is abundant sinning. It simply means that God can accomplish His best even when man does his worst. There's an old saying: "When God cannot rule, God will overrule, but He will always accomplish His purpose." God didn't choose the decision of Abram and Sarai; they acted outside the spectrum of His will. But God did overrule and intervene so that His plan continued to unfold unhindered.

God will always accomplish His purpose—but why take the long way around? Why live so poorly that you end up saying, "Yeah, I messed up, but I'm glad God was there to pick up the pieces. And then I'm going to mess up tomorrow and say the same thing, and mess up again next week"? We all mess up, of course; but why keep taking the long way around? Why allow circumstances to slow us down? Why not cooperate with God from the beginning, so that we leave a positive legacy and make a wonderful mark on the world?

Let God Help You

When we take trips these days, most of us drive. But to drive safely, we have to concentrate on the road ahead and avoid distractions. Can you guess the number-one driving distraction?

An insurance company took a survey of thousands of drivers around the country and found several distractions that rank high on the list. Twenty-nine percent of drivers surveyed listed using their cell phone as a distraction. Fifty-seven percent said they ate while driving. Sixty-two percent named tuning the radio as a distraction.

And the number-one offender? Drinking coffee. Do you know why? Because coffee is fluid. It can move and tends to spill. Most drivers said the biggest distraction occurred early in the morning, on their way to work, when a full cup of coffee spilled on their work clothes. Because of the spill, they had to pull over to the side of the road or go home to change clothes.

Imagine somebody trying to cram breakfast, a stop at Starbucks, a trip to work, and maybe even putting on makeup, all while driving. We think, *If I do it all at one time and cram it in and push, push, push—I'll get it all done quickly.* But then the coffee spills, our work clothes are soaked, we have to go home to change, and we end up late for work.

A detour like that can take you much, much longer than sticking to the main road. It'll take you long way around and cause you more anxiety and trouble than you ever expected. If you pick the wrong day to arrive late for work, it could even cost you your job.

Vance Havner had it right: "The detour is always worse than the main road."

I'll bet you've heard the saying, "God helps those who help themselves." Some people think the saying comes from the Bible. In fact, I grew up hearing people insist, "The Bible says, 'God helps those who help themselves.'" But I've read my Bible in several translations, and I have to tell you: it's not in there.

We call this a phantom verse. Jesus never said it, the apostles never said it, and none of the prophets ever said it. Do you know who said it? Benjamin Franklin. You won't find it in the Bible anywhere.

Too many followers of Christ accept the common misconception that if they plan, strategize, and move, God will somehow, someday, catch up with them and carry them along. He'll help them if they first help themselves.

But what if they're doing something outside His will? What if they're taking a disastrous detour, like Abram and Sarai? Is it worth taking the long way around?

Nope.

The best route is always God's route. The plan of our Lord—even when it seems to take an awfully long time to unfold—will always turn out far better than anything we might devise on our own.

So listen carefully to God's promises. Wait patiently for them to happen. And seek diligently to bring Him glory. That's the way to make your mark on the world and leave it a better place than you found it.

MEDITATING ON THE MARK

In this chapter we learned that, despite the old saying, God doesn't help those who help themselves; He helps those who seek His help. In seeking the will of God, there are four mile markers: vulnerability, impetuosity, legacy, and epiphany.

Vulnerability. Abram and Sarai were waiting on God and His promise that she would bear a child. Are you waiting on God for anything today? Be honest. Could you wait on God for eleven or more years concerning this matter? Sarai did.

Impetuosity. Sarai decided to take matters into her own hands. Can you think back on a time when you failed to wait on God? What were the results?

Legacy. Because of Abram and Sarai's plotting and planning on behalf of God, Hagar gave birth to Ishmael. This legacy is what the couple reaped from God. What were the international ramifications of their decision? What is going on right now in the Arab-Israeli conflict?

Epiphany. This is God's merciful and gracious intervention. When did God pursue you in spite of your abandonment of Him? When did He bless you in spite of your disobedience?

MODELING THE MASTER'S MARK

Vulnerability. Isaiah 40:31: *"But those who wait on the LORD shall renew their strength; they shall mount up with wings like eagles, they shall run and not be weary, they shall walk and not faint."*

Impetuosity. Psalm 40:1: *"I waited patiently for the LORD; and He inclined to me, and heard my cry."*

Legacy. Mark 13:8: *"For nation will rise against nation, and kingdom against kingdom.... These are the beginnings of sorrows."*

Epiphany. Deuteronomy 28:2: *"And all these blessings shall come upon you and overtake you, because you obey the voice of the LORD your God."*

MAKING YOUR MARK

Are you pursuing your own personal goals, or are you working for the glory of God? This week, give God alone the glory as you drop off clothes at a donation center and groceries at your local food bank.

CHAPTER EIGHT

A New Start for an Old Soldier

Some time ago I found an article titled, "The Perks of Being Over Fifty." For Abram's sake, however, I think we should say, "The Perks of Being Almost One Hundred." Consider the top ten:

1. Kidnappers are not very interested in you.
2. In hostage situations you're likely to be released first.
3. People call at 9 P.M. and ask, "Did I wake you?"
4. There's nothing left to learn the hard way.
5. You can eat dinner at 4:00 P.M.
6. You enjoy hearing about other people's operations.
7. You have a party and the neighbors don't even realize it.
8. You quit trying to hold your stomach in, no matter who walks into the room.
9. You sing along with elevator music.
10. Your secrets are safe with your friends—they can't remember them, either.[1]

I find it interesting how we determine age. When our children are very young, we measure age in months. "She's seventeen months, four days, and three hours old." As they get a little past that stage, we start monitoring their age in half years. Kids often say, "I'm five and a half," and it's important to them that you recognize that half. Soon after, we move into full years. Next, we don't want to tell our exact age, so we start reporting our age in decades. "I'm in my thirties." And finally we reach an age where nobody even bothers to ask.

Unlike our custom, the Bible tells us exactly how old Abraham is in the very first verse of Genesis 17: *"When Abram was ninety-nine years old."*

Chapter 17 marks a brand-new beginning for Abram. The Bible tells us he hasn't heard from God for thirteen years, ever since the Hagar incident. Since that time, he's apparently endured a long, quiet period of 156 silent months. We don't read of God speaking to Abram in that time—not even once.

Let's not miss out on the significance of that silent period. We must realize that the Christian life is not an ongoing, spectacular array of the eventful and the miraculous. Some people expect a heavenly visitation every day or two. If that's you, then you're in for some big disappointments. Whether or not we admit it, the typical Christian life has its routine and even mundane silences as we walk by faith and not by sight.

At his advanced age, Abram might have thought the time had come to take up lawn bowling. But by God's grace, he marked his one-hundredth birthday by ushering in something entirely new. We don't normally associate the word "new" with someone ninety-nine years old—maybe a new will, maybe a new hearing aid, or new dentures—but not things like a new car.

And certainly not a new son.

But Abram would welcome a son into his world at the ripe old age of one hundred. And so began the next phase of this man's life. Let's look at four of his new experiences.

El Shaddai

When Abram was ninety-nine years old, the LORD appeared to Abram and said to him, "I am Almighty God; walk before Me and be blameless." (Genesis 17:1)

The name "Almighty God" translates as the Hebrew term *El Shaddai,* a very important designation of God in the Scripture. Of the forty-eight times this title occurs in the Old Testament, this is the very first appearance.

No one knows the true origin of the term. The original may have come from an Akkadian word that meant "mountain" or "breast." When you look at the horizon and see a mountain rising from the ground, it looks something like a strong chest muscle flexing its strength.

When God calls Himself El Shaddai, Almighty God, He means that He is the all-sufficient one. He is the divinely buff one. He can do anything. That's how God introduces himself to Abram in this chapter. In verse 4 God says, *"As for Me, behold, My covenant is with you."* The phrase "as for me" is generally used in the Hebrew language as an emphatic self-reference, drawing all attention upon the speaker. Throughout this chapter, God himself takes center stage.

Why would God—after thirteen years of apparent silence—introduce himself to Abram in this way? After we read the rest of the chapter, it seems easy enough to figure out. God will inform Abram that his geriatric wife (who isn't much younger than he is) will have a son within a year. Since the birth is clearly a miracle, he calls himself El Shaddai.

Twelve times in this passage, God uses the term, "I will." "I will do this," "I will do that." Do you think He's trying to make a point? By repeating the idea a dozen times, He makes it emphatic that He is going to do something. And when He sets out to do something, expect the amazing. Paul wrote: *"Now to Him who is able to do exceedingly abundantly above all that we ask or think"* (Ephesians 3:20). God is no weakling. He does not operate in reserve mode with His power; He operates at full strength at all times. Scripture says: *"I know that You can do everything, and that no purpose of Yours can be withheld from You"* (Job 42:2).

James Smith wrote a great set of books called *Handfuls of Purpose: Outline Studies on the Old Testament.* He said, "This promise of God, this is the divine plaster large enough to cover any human sore." Whatever difficulty you might be facing, whatever burden you might be carrying, God is almighty and all-sufficient. He has more than enough divine plaster to cover you.

There's another reason why God came to Abram at this point in his life. He's ninety-nine, which would make Ishmael thirteen years old. I think Abram began to settle into the modus operandi of, "This is my boy. God promised me a son, and this is the one. I'm satisfied. This is as far as it goes." Abram probably got used to the idea of Ishmael being the promised heir.

Abram really did think along these lines: consider how he responded to God's revelation that Sarai would bear him a son. Abram laughed aloud and said, *"Oh, that Ishmael might live before You!"* (Genesis 17:18). In other words, "God, you are so gracious; but really, this is enough for me. I have Ishmael. Let him be the fulfillment of your promise."

Maybe Abram took a long walk one evening with his son. He looked at his boy and felt sure that this child was it for him. Perhaps he looked back over a dozen years and thought, *Oh, those days so long ago when God used to speak to me! How sweet that was. And that promise that He made about a son—well, here's the fulfillment of that promise, I suppose.* And perhaps at that very moment God spoke to him: "I am El Shaddai. I'm going to make my covenant with you—and with Sarai."

Proverbs 5:21 says: *"For the ways of man are before the eyes of the LORD, and He ponders all his paths."* And Proverbs 16:9 adds: *"A man's heart plans his way, but the LORD directs his steps."*

One evening many years ago a minister listening to his CB radio heard a trucker driving through town trying to contact a prostitute. The trucker got no response on his CB. He tried again. No response. Finally he said, "Well, sorry I missed you. I'll try to contact you next time I go through town." The minister picked up his CB and said, "She may not have heard you, but God did." After a long pause, the trucker replied, "You know, I knew this CB had good range, but I didn't know it was that good." No thought crosses your mind that God doesn't already completely know. And in some way, He responds to it. God knew Abram needed a new revelation of himself because He knew the man's thoughts. And so He re-introduced himself by His great name: El Shaddai—Almighty God.

But Abram needed more than a new revelation; he also needed a new commission. So God gave him that, too.

Walk Before Me

God instructed Abram, "Walk before Me and be blameless." Never before had the Lord spoken these words to Abram. What did He mean by them?

When you "walk before" someone, you walk in plain view of that person. But the phrase here means more than simply walking in plain view of someone else. It means that while you walk, you know you're doing it in plain view of that person. You recognize that the individual is watching you.

If you're a parent, you've noticed how your kids act when they know you're in the room. Sometimes they look to see if you've left; and if they think you have, they may start acting differently.

It's something like that with Abram. God says to him, "Walk before Me, Abram." That is, "Live your life, conduct your business, and make your choices, realizing that you do it all in My sight. Don't walk before the world. Don't walk before your family. Walk before Me—first and foremost."

The Lord also said to Abram, "... *and be blameless.*" God didn't require moral perfection of him, of course, because Abram had a fallen nature, just as we do. And in these fallen bodies of ours, frankly it's impossible to live a morally perfect life. Instead, the idea is wholehearted, undivided devotion. "As you walk before Me, Abram, keep your eyes locked on Me—just Me—with wholehearted devotion." That's what King Hezekiah confessed to God: *"Remember now, O LORD, I pray, how I have walked before You in truth and with a loyal heart"* (2 Kings 20:3).

But why would God choose this time—when Abram was ninety-nine years old—to give him this command? I think it was because Abram's spiritual life to this point had lurched and sputtered sporadically. It had not been blameless.

Abram didn't walk before God blamelessly when he stopped in Haran for fifteen years, instead of moving immediately to Canaan.

He didn't walk wholeheartedly before God when he fled to Egypt because of a famine in Canaan.

He didn't walk before God blamelessly when he lied to Pharaoh about his wife and said, "She's my sister."

He didn't walk before God in wholehearted devotion in the Hagar and Ishmael incident. Instead, he walked before Sarai and let her do whatever she wanted.

Nevertheless, God said to Abram, "I am Almighty God. You're ninety-nine. It's high time that you grew up. It's time for you to start walking before Me. Be blameless."

In other words, "I'm giving you a new start, Abram."

As we read through Scripture, not once do we see God rehearsing Abram's failures. He didn't say, "Abram, walk before Me and be blameless, because we all know how often you've failed." In fact, as we read the New Testament, we notice that none of Abram's failures are mentioned once. Rather, the Bible lifts him up as a preeminent example of faith.

In the New Testament, we read: *"By faith Abraham obeyed when he was called to go out to the place which he would receive as an inheritance. And he went out, not knowing where he was going"* (Hebrews 11:8). Did Abram obey? Well, yes, eventually. But the New Testament only says that he obeyed. It leaves out the other part.

Truly, our God is the God of the second chance—and of the third chance and of the eighty-fourth chance. Abram failed time and again, but falling down isn't the issue. It's staying down. Each time Abram got back up and started over. With God, it's never three strikes and you're out—He'll give you a whole new at-bat.

Paul wrote that love *"thinks no evil,"* or as a different translation says, love *"keeps no record of wrongs"* (1 Corinthians 13:5, NIV). Of course, God knows our faults. He remembers. But He chooses to deal with you and me without regard to our rebellious pasts.

A husband and wife visited a counselor's office. Immediately the husband began explaining the problem from his perspective. "Whenever we have an argument," he said, "my wife gets so historical." The counselor smiled in a condescending way, flashing an "I'm smart and you just said something dumb" look.

"I think you mean, she acts 'hysterical,'" he replied.

"Oh, no, sir," the man insisted. "I mean she's historical. She's always digging up my past."

God will never dig up the past with His children. If you've trusted Christ for your salvation, He will always see you through His loving eyes. And that explains why He chose to remain silent about Abram's gaffes throughout the rest of Scripture.

All of us can start over, have a fresh beginning, and enjoy a new walk with God—at any age. Abram had reached ninety-nine, but God still told him, "It's time to walk before Me and be blameless, Abram."

"You mean I get a new start, even at this late time of my life?"

Definitely.

You can start over at any age—but you have to make that choice.

Someone once said there are four ages of man. The first is when you believe in Santa Claus. The second is when you stop believing in Santa Claus. The third is when you are Santa Claus. And the fourth is when you look like Santa Claus.[2]

Abram must have looked a lot like Santa Claus—but he was just learning the right way to walk. Don't ever think, *Oh, I'm too old for that.*

Moses was eighty when he began his work as the deliverer.

Caleb was eighty-five when he began his pioneering adventure in Hebron.

Golda Meier was seventy-one when she became prime minister of Israel.

Ronald Reagan was seventy-seven when he finished his service as President of the United States.

Benjamin Franklin was eighty-one when he helped frame the U.S. Constitution.

And Abram got his new start at age ninety-nine.

Any age!

New Names

Perhaps to emphasize that He had begun a new work in Abram's life, the Lord gave Abram a new name: *"No longer shall your name be called Abram, but your name shall be Abraham; for I have made you a father of many nations"* (Genesis 17:5). God did the same thing for Sarai: *"As for Sarai your wife, you shall not call her name Sarai, but Sarah shall be her name ... and she shall be a mother of nations; kings of peoples shall be from her"* (Genesis 17:15-16).

In the Bible, new names indicate new directions. Jesus gave Simon the new name of Peter. Moses renamed Hoshea ("deliverer") Yahoshua ("God is my deliverer"). Christians in India take on Christian names when they get baptized. And the Puritans used to do the same thing. So what did God mean by giving Abram the new name of Abraham?

First, we should understand that Abram means, "exalted father." I'm sure Abram took a lot of abuse for that name during all the years he had no children. The day Ishmael came along, he probably said, "Whew! Now I can finally get some respect." But then God came to him and said, "Just when you got used to your old name, Mr. Exalted Father, I'm giving you a new one. From now on you'll be called Abraham—because I'm going to make you Mr. Father of a Multitude. How do you like that?"

I bet Abraham replied, "God, please. If you love me, can you choose another name? I've already put up with the first one for a long time."

But the new name stuck, and we've known him as Abraham ever since.

Some people have names that seem to fit them perfectly. The dentist I had growing up didn't believe in using much pain medication, which explains why his name was Dr. Steel (as in, "nerves of").

Other people have names that don't fit them at all. An attorney named Grace just doesn't work. A braggart named George Meek? Doesn't fit. And Abraham—"Father of a Multitude"—seems a highly unlikely fit for this old guy.

Imagine a caravan snaking through Canaan after doing business in Egypt. Abraham hasn't been to Egypt for years, but the men of the caravan recognize him.

"Hey there! You're the 'Exalted Father' we met in Egypt, aren't you?" They pause, sneer at him, and ask, "Is that your boy?"

"Yes," Abraham says proudly. "His name is Ishmael."

"Well, congratulations, Mr. Exalted Father."

"Thanks—but that's not my name anymore. My new name is 'Father of a Multitude.'"

You can almost hear the uproarious laughter. It must've been tough for old Abraham.

Why the name change? And why now? Why call him Abraham before Isaac and the rest of his children are born? Why not afterward?

I believe that Ishmael was Abram and Sarai's way of exalting themselves. "I'm 'Exalted Father.' I did this my way. Here's my son." When God renamed Abram "Father of a Multitude," He put a goal so out of reach for Abraham that he could never fulfill it on his own. God intended to stretch Abraham's faith. He stretched it by first declaring His purpose—only later would He fulfill it.

And what about Sarai's name change? Sarai means "contentious," "dominant," or "domineering." I don't know what her folks were thinking. Can you imagine what life in a home with contentious, domineering Sarai must have felt like? *Better to dwell in the wilderness,* says Proverbs 21:19, *"than with a contentious and angry woman."*

Sarai had to feel very happy the day God changed her name to Sarah, which means "princess." You can almost hear her joy: "Oh, thank you, Lord!" The Talmud, an ancient Jewish commentary, says the name change symbolized the end of Sarah's barrenness, since within a year she would have a child. The New Testament never calls Abraham's wife Sarai; she is always referred to as Sarah. In fact, Peter mentions Sarah as the model of a godly, submissive woman. (See 1 Peter 3:6.)

Our relationship with God should always move forward and progress; it should never stagnate. We should be continually advancing, spiritually speaking. I doubt we can have regular contact with the living God and stay the same. It's impossible. If we walk before a living God who is both all-powerful and almighty, then we must see some progress and changes in our lives. Remember, He's the one who said, *"Behold, I make all things new"* (Revelation 21:5).

You probably know that most college athletic teams name themselves after ferocious animals—eagles, bears, cougars. If God were to give you a nickname, based upon your spiritual characteristics, what He would call you? What animal you would most resemble?

A bear?

An eagle?

A goldfish?

A tapeworm?

There are a ton of possibilities, aren't there?

What do you think God would like to do with you? What name would He give you? What changes would He want to bring into your life?

He took Abram and made him into Abraham.

He took Sarai and made her into Sarah.

What would God like to make of you? Think about it.

He Remains Faithful

In Genesis 17 the Bible uses the word covenant nine times. God said to Abraham, *"And I will make My covenant between Me and you, and will multiply you exceedingly.... I will make you exceedingly fruitful"* (Genesis 17:2; 6). We have heard very similar words before, haven't we? God promised to make nations come from Abraham, to give his descendants the Promised Land forever, and to eternally remain the God of His people.

Many years before, God established His covenant with Abraham. This time, He chose to make a new declaration of the Old Covenant. Perhaps Abraham started thinking that the covenant promise had come to an end: Here's Ishmael. That's all there is. To make sure that Abraham wouldn't jump to any conclusions, God renewed the covenant. It's a bit like a boy or girl at summer camp might renew a commitment to the Lord, or as couples married for decades renew their wedding vows in a special ceremony.

The Abrahamic Covenant centers on the land of Israel and the chosen people of God. The Lord laid out its features in Genesis chapters 12, 13, 15, and again here in chapter 17. He was saying, "Abram, you and your descendants will own that land in the Middle East—forever." Of course, the ultimate fulfillment came in Jesus Christ, because through this covenant all the nations of the world would be blessed. So Paul wrote:

> *That the blessing of Abraham might come upon the Gentiles in Christ Jesus.... Now to Abraham and his Seed were the promises made. He does not say, "And to seeds," as of many, but as of one, "And to your Seed," who is Christ.* (Galatians 3:14, 16)

How amazing that—to a man with such a checkered past and a history of failure—God promised another staggering blessing.

Did you know that God deals the same way with you and me? Even when we behave badly (and how often are we really on our best behavior?), God promises to stay faithful. Paul wrote: *"If we are faithless, He remains faithful; He cannot deny Himself"* (2 Timothy 2:13).

Even though Abram was faithless when—after God told him to leave—he remained in Haran for fifteen years, God still blessed him.

Even when Abram had a lapse of faith—fleeing to Egypt because of a famine in Canaan—God didn't negate His blessings and promises.

Even though Abram lied to Pharaoh about his wife, his sin couldn't abrogate the blessings and promises of God.

Even when Abram's impatience with God led him to have a son by Hagar and not Sarai—God didn't stop blessing him.

What a mighty God who deals with us!

In the Dust

Abraham stood in awe of all that God promised to do for him and he responded with a new submission. Like we all should.

It's not easy for a ninety-nine-year-old man to fall on his knees, but Abraham did. He sank to the ground and, there in the dust, God spoke with him. Abraham had not enjoyed such sweet fellowship with his Lord for a very long time. He may have fallen on his face in absolute joy. He's back! He's talking to me again! He's not done with me yet! I'm an old guy, but God has given me new hope.

That's true worship.

True worship always responds to the true revelation of God. You don't have to "work up" true worship. It doesn't come in a burst of the moment. True worship responds to the Person, character, and the revelation of God—with exuberance and joy.

I've Growed!

Howard Hendricks, longtime professor at Dallas Theological Seminary, once told about leaving home for a two-week mission trip. Before he left, his second daughter, Bev, said to him, "Daddy, while you're gone, I promise I'll grow."

"Okay, honey, great," he replied.

As soon as he got off the airplane when he arrived home, she ran to him and said, "Daddy, Daddy! Quick, come home. Let's see how much I've growed!"

So father and daughter went to the door in the closet where they marked off her changes in height. If she had grown at all, he said, maybe it was a couple of millimeters; but they marked it anyway. She was so happy.

"See, I told you I growed!" Bev beamed, jumping up and down. "I've growed!"

They walked into the living room, where she asked one of those kid questions that make most parents uncomfortable.

"Daddy," she asked, "why do big people stop growing?"

Why do big people stop growing? You can explain to a child, "Well, they stop growing up, but they continue to grow out. Like a nice dresser, the middle drawer stays open." In one way or another, we never stop growing physically.

But have you stopped growing, stretching, and moving in your spiritual life?

"Oh, I'm too old for that."

Really?

When a man turns sixty, what does he usually do? Most men retire—or they'd like to. They throw a big party. Not Larry Elmore, a former airline pilot from Florida. Larry faced mandatory retirement at age sixty, so to mark that milestone he decided to parachute from an airplane sixty times in one day.[3]

Growing old is inevitable. Growing up is optional.

What new thing is God stirring within your heart? Are you growing in your relationship with the Lord? Regardless of your age, you never have to stop growing, stretching, and moving spiritually. As Abram—let's make that Abraham—discovered, life began at age ninety-nine. And it only got better from there.

MEDITATING ON THE MARK

In this chapter we learned that the Christian life is not filled with unbelievable miracles and inconceivable events every day. Instead, we are to walk by faith and not by sight. Abram's new life (at ninety-nine years of age) was commemorated by four new experiences: revelation, commission, designation, and declaration.

Revelation. God introduced himself to Abram as "El Shaddai," the Almighty God. He is the most sufficient One; He can do anything. How do you put your own limits on God? How do you resist His power?

Commission. Abram was given clear instructions from God: "Walk before Me and be blameless." Are you living your life completely aware that everything is in His sight?

Designation. At the age of ninety-nine, Abram received a new name: Abraham. His new name indicates a change of direction for him. As a Christian, are you moving forward spiritually? Or is your relationship with God stagnant?

Declaration. Although Abraham didn't have a perfect past, God renewed His covenant with him and promised His blessings. How do you feel knowing that God promises to stay faithful to you even when you are not faithful to Him?

MODELING THE MASTER'S MARK

Revelation. Psalm 62:11: *"Twice I have heard this: that power belongs to God."*

Commission. Micah 6:8: *"And what does the LORD require of you but to do justly, to love mercy, and to walk humbly with your God?"*

Designation. 1 Peter 2:2-3: *"As newborn babes, desire the pure milk of the word, that you may grow thereby."*

Declaration. 1 John 1:9: *"If we confess our sins, He is faithful and just to forgive us our sins and to cleanse us from all unrighteousness."*

MAKING YOUR MARK

Each day this week, determine to spend seven minutes in wholehearted, undivided, distraction-free devotion to God.

CHAPTER NINE

Before God Makes His Mark

Many of us live too much of our lives in the sleepy mode of "just getting by." We don't live in excellence. We live in mediocrity.

Natalie Gabal reminds us of the consequences of settling for "good enough." What happens when we go for excellence just 99 percent of the time? If we all settled for mediocrity, even just 1 percent of the time:

This year alone, the IRS would lose two million documents.

Each day twelve babies would go to the wrong parents.

Two hundred ninety-one pacemaker operations would go awry.

Pharmacists would write twenty thousand incorrect drug prescriptions.

Manufacturers would ship 114,500 mismatched pairs of shoes.[1]

Keep in mind, that's living with just a little bit of mediocrity. Isaac Disraeli said, "It's a wretched waste of time to be gratified with mediocrity when the excellent lies before us."

A young naval ensign took his first cruise overseas. When the ship headed back toward the United States, his turn came to command the vessel. He was so excited! He spouted out commands, got the ship's deck buzzing with activity, and managed to get the huge ship sailing out of the foreign port and back to the U.S. He did it in record time.

As the destroyer sped toward America, a seaman walked up to the ensign with a note from the captain. The young ensign was surprised. The note read simply, "My personal congratulations. You completed the exercise according to the book at amazing speed. However, in your haste, you overlooked one of the unwritten rules: Make sure the captain is aboard before getting underway."[2]

As Abram discovered, haste often has a way of undermining excellence. God wanted this man to live with excellence. He wanted Abram to make his mark on the world, and eventually he did. But before that could happen, God had to make His mark on Abram's life. Abram had to learn and act on the three prerequisites to making his mark on the world—and the same apply to us.

Promises, Promises

If you want to live with excellence and make a significant mark on your world, then make sure that God is onboard and calling the shots. And that you're actively listening to Him.

Three times in Genesis 17 we read of God speaking to Abram, and for eleven verses we read of Abram listening to what God wanted to say. That means that God spoke a great deal into Abram's life. But it also means that Abram accepted His words.

God first told Abraham that he had to keep the covenant given to him by circumcising himself and every male born in his household. Abram's descendants throughout history were to do the same. Now, try to picture Abraham as he listens to these divine instructions—and don't forget that he's ninety-nine years old.

Every male child among you shall be circumcised; and you shall be circumcised in the flesh of your foreskins, and it shall be a sign of the covenant between Me and you. He who is eight days old among you shall be circumcised, every male child in your generations, he who is born in your house or bought with money from any foreigner who is not your descendant. He who is born in your house and he who is bought with your money must be circumcised, and My covenant shall be in your flesh for an everlasting covenant. (Genesis 17:10-13)

In the ancient world, the greater of the two parties making a covenant always set the terms. We see the same pattern here. Because God was—clearly—the greater partner in this covenant, He established the terms. One of those terms involved a sign, or a token, of the covenant. As a Semite, Abraham knew all about covenants. He knew that every contract (and a covenant is a contract) had to be sealed with a token, with some outward demonstration of the covenant.

When God gave Noah a covenant, He placed a rainbow in the sky—a colorful, beautiful, visible token of the contract: *"Never again shall all flesh be cut off by the waters of the flood; never again shall there be a flood to destroy the earth"* (Genesis 9:11).

Centuries later when God—through Moses—affirmed the covenant of the Law, he gave Israel a different sign: Shabbat, the Sabbath, was a token signifying peace and rest.

When Jesus established a new covenant in the New Testament, He also provided a sign for the redeemed: baptism—a cleansing, a refreshing.

Even in marriage, a husband gives his bride a token— usually a diamond ring—to signify the contract of marriage.

That's the outward sign of the covenant. It's brilliant. It's beautiful. It's thoughtful.

It's expensive.

Abram knew all about covenants. As he waited to see what sign God would give him to close the covenant, he must have wondered what it might be: Will it be some angelic apparition or maybe a sign in the sky, like Noah?

Picture Abraham smiling and eagerly waiting for this gift. Suddenly God whispers to him—and Abraham's face grows pale.

"What?!" he exclaims.

"You got it, buddy," God answers. "Both you and your male descendants must be circumcised."

Keep in mind that Abraham is just one year shy of a century. He must have thought:

Nobody told me that old age would be this tough. I never dreamed God would come up with this kind of arrangement. It was great when God said, "I'll bless you. I'll make you a blessing and I'll give you this and that." But I don't really like this token.

We don't always like what God has to say to us, do we? Sometimes God speaks things that are difficult to hear. But if we want to make our mark on the world, then we have to listen carefully to everything He says. It's the only way.

But we all tend to gravitate toward certain promises in the Bible. We'll highlight them in yellow, orange, and purple. We write notes by them and record dates when God moved in power. But we usually avoid other promises of Scripture—equally applicable to us—that speak of hardship and pain and difficult times. We love the verses that promise us stuff:

Now to Him who is able to keep you from stumbling. (Jude 1:24)

Now to Him who is able to do exceedingly abundantly above all that we ask or think. (Ephesians 3:20)

And my God shall supply all your need. (Philippians 4:19)

Come to Me, all you who labor and are heavy laden, and I will give you rest. (Matthew 11:28)

If I asked you to open your Bible, I'll bet that I would find a number of these promises underlined. That's good—they should be.

But few of us spend half as much time highlighting other promises:

In the world you will have tribulation. (John 16:33)

Behold, I send you out as sheep in the midst of wolves. (Matthew 10:16)

And you will be hated by all for My name's sake. (Matthew 10:22)

All who desire to live godly in Christ Jesus will suffer persecution. (2 Timothy 3:12)

You might read those and say, "Wait a minute. I didn't bargain for that. I didn't sign up for that. What about 'God loves you and has a wonderful plan for your life'?" Are those passages underlined in your Bible?

When we come face-to-face with Scripture's darker promises and hear God speaking words that we don't especially want to hear, some of us come to a foolish decision. We would never dream of admitting it, but our lives reveal it anyway: "I will not allow God to speak into my life. I will take what I want and disregard the rest."

These kinds of Christians devise clever barriers to keep their ears from hearing whatever makes them feel uncomfortable. They read the passages they like and avoid those they don't. They devour soft, easy books, but stay away from edgy, exhortative works. They'll visit a counselor whom they believe will tell them exactly what they want to hear, but avoid anyone who will tell them the hard truth. They will listen to a sermon only so far, and when it gets a tad unnerving, they'll tune out or walk out.

To what degree will you allow God to speak His truth into your life? And how fully will you permit God to use others to hold you accountable? Do you invite friends to correct you when necessary?

Do you know what often happens when such loving confrontation occurs? The confronted say things like, "Don't be so legalistic. What gives you the right to judge me? Jesus wouldn't do that."

We construct all sorts of clever barriers to keep God out.

A classic example of selective hearing occurs in John's Gospel. As long as Jesus healed the sick and gave the hungry free bread, people flocked to Him for more. But when He started speaking truths that they found difficult to understand, or instructions they disliked, they quickly turned away. John writes simply, *"From that time many of His disciples went back and walked with Him no more"* (John 6:66). We say these folks were believers, but not belongers. "I'll follow you anywhere, Jesus!" they probably said. "As long as you tell me what I want to hear. But if I don't like it, I'm going somewhere else."

How can God speak into anyone's life with that kind of attitude? Can you honestly say to God, "You can tell me anything because you are the Lord"?

Let's press this idea: God speaks primarily through His Word. Are you attending a Christ-centered church where you regularly hear His Word preached? What's your attitude?

My wife makes me go.

My parents promised me I'd get my allowance if I showed up—so I'm here.

I wouldn't miss it.

What's your attitude?

Paul wrote to Timothy:

> *Preach the word! Be ready in season and out of season. Convince, rebuke, exhort, with all longsuffering and teaching. For the time will come when they will not endure sound doctrine, but according to their own desires, because they have itching ears, they will heap up for themselves teachers; and they will turn their ears away from the truth, and be turned aside to fables.* (2 Timothy 4:2-4)

Does listening to the Word hurt? Sometimes it does. It can hurt a lot. When Scripture penetrates to the heart, it can "cut to the quick." The writer of Hebrews declared:

> *For the word of God is living and powerful, and sharper than any two-edged sword, piercing even to the division of soul and spirit, and of joints and marrow, and is a discerner of the thoughts and intents of the heart. And there is no creature hidden from His sight, but all things are naked and open to the eyes of Him to whom we must give account.* (Hebrews 4:12-13)

The word "open" comes from the Greek *trakelidzo*, where we get the word trachea—the throat. It means "to lay bare." The idea goes back to Old Testament sacrificial days. When a priest made a sacrifice, he would pull back the lamb's neck, stretch it, and run his blade across the jugular, bleeding the animal to death.

God's Word often goes for the jugular, doesn't it? That's why some sermons comfort the afflicted—and afflict the comfortable.

If we want to make our mark, we have to allow God to speak His truth into our lives. No matter what He wants to say to us. We can't build up barriers, tune out uncomfortable ideas, or think the passage is for somebody else. Instead, we must learn to ask, "God, what are you trying to tell me?"

Some people have told me, "Skip, God doesn't speak like He used to."

I disagree. I think people don't listen like they used to.

A pair of authors wrote:

> Many irregular church attendees consistently focus their minds on sporting events, business affairs, or matters of personal interest as soon as the sermon begins. Many so-called worshipers can tell you what dress that pastor's wife wore in the service, but they cannot recall the text of the sermon or the application of the message in their lives.[3]

Do you want to make your mark in life? Honestly? If so, then let God's Word penetrate all the way to your heart. Without meeting that prerequisite, you can't get any further.

Re-what?

On the same day that God gave Abraham the rite of circumcision as the sign of His covenant, Abraham obeyed. He not only circumcised himself—at age ninety-nine—he also circumcised thirteen-year-old Ishmael and every other male in his household.

Abraham may have felt uncomfortable with the idea of circumcision, but he certainly knew about it. Many of the surrounding nations practiced circumcision. The Ammonites, the Moabites, and even the sixth dynasty of the Egyptians practiced it, as did the sons of some Roman priests. We don't know exactly why they practiced it; some say for hygienic purposes, others suggest it was to ward off demons. We do know why ancient Israel practiced circumcision: God gave it to Abraham as a sign of the covenant, both for himself and for all his descendants. In Moses' day it became part of the Law. The Jews call it the *berit milah*, or the "symbol of the covenant."

God told Abraham, *"My covenant shall be in your flesh"* (Genesis 17:13). In other words, "Abraham, here is an outward action for you to take to display an inward truth. I want you to portray, through a visible sign, an invisible reality." God intended the outward symbol of circumcision to portray faith in the Lord and repentance toward Him. Through the sign of circumcision, those who received it were saying, "I believe in God and so I have cut away the flesh—the sin—in my life." Paul wrote, *"And he received the sign of circumcision, a seal of the righteousness of the faith which he had while still uncircumcised"* (Romans 4:11). Circumcision represented the cutting away of a life lived according to one's own desires in order to pursue a life of repentance and faith.

Unfortunately, the descendants of Abraham (and especially post-biblical Jews) made more out of circumcision than God had intended. It was turned from a symbol into a sacrament. And there's a big difference. The former signifies truth; the latter suggests that the rite itself conveys some spiritual blessing. The Talmud states, "If an Israelite practices idolatry, he is going to hell; but before he goes to hell, his circumcision shall be first removed." In other words, God would somehow surgically reverse the circumcision before sending a fallen Jew to eternal punishment. Some rabbis even ascribed circumcision to Adam, Seth, Noah, and Melchizedek, although the Bible nowhere suggests such an idea.

The Zohar, the most mystical book in extra-biblical Judaism, says, "As long as Israel observes the custom of circumcision, Heaven and Earth will go on their appointed courses; but if Israel neglects that covenant, Heaven and Earth will be disturbed." In other words, if the descendants of Abraham ever discontinued the sign of circumcision, the world would somehow change.

Do you see the problem with taking a legitimate symbol and making it into something more than God intended? When you do that, it becomes easy to substitute the symbol of circumcision for the reality of repentance.

We know that God intended the symbol as something that spoke much more deeply than the outward act. Several times in the Old Testament, God gave a similar warning: *"Therefore circumcise the foreskin of your heart, and be stiff-necked no longer"* (Deuteronomy 10:16). God designed circumcision to remind His people of their ongoing need to repent and return to faith in Him.

When my wife first gave her life to Christ, all she did was read a "Four Spiritual Laws" tract, bow her head, and say, "Okay, Jesus, come inside and give me all this stuff that you promised." One day as she listened to a sermon at Calvary Chapel in Costa Mesa, California, she felt very uneasy. She went into the prayer room and told a counselor, "I prayed this prayer, but I feel something's wrong." The counselor happened to be my British friend, Malcolm Wilde.

"Have you repented of your sins?" he asked her.

"Have I what?" she replied.

"Have you repented of your sins?"

"Re-what?"

And then Malcolm explained the idea of cutting off the old and turning to Jesus Christ.

Why do we so seldom preach repentance these days? Wasn't it the hallmark of the ministries of both Jesus and John the Baptist?

Many of us today don't like to accept the reality of personal sin. In fact, we don't even like the word sin. We won't use it. "Oh, that word is so out," we say. We prefer hang-ups, issues, mistakes, alternative lifestyles, problems, brokenness.

A little book called *The Politically Correct Dictionary* cleverly renames common things. It calls a shoplifter "a nontraditional shopper." A serial killer becomes "a person with difficult-to-meet needs." Evil is renamed "morally different," and a drunk is called "chemically inconvenienced."

But changing the name of sin doesn't alter its destructive character. *"For the wages of sin is death"* (Romans 6:23). Sin kills. That's why God insists that we repent of it.

Paul Harvey once told a story of how Eskimos kill wolves. He said that the Eskimo coats the knife's blade with animal blood and lets it freeze. Then he adds another layer of blood, freezes it, and then another. As each coat freezes, he adds another smear of blood until the blade hides underneath a substantial thickness of frozen blood. Finally he buries the handle of the knife, with the blade up.

In the frozen tundra, the wolf catches the scent of fresh blood on the knife and begins to lick it. He licks it more and more until the blade is bare. Because of the cold, the wolf never notices the pain of the blade as it slices his tongue. His ferocious craving for the taste of blood prevents him from realizing that he is satisfying his thirst by licking up his own warm blood. He licks the blade until he bleeds to death. He never recognizes that he is swallowing his own life.

What a perfect analogy of sin. That's exactly what it does. It tastes so good, and you go for it—but all the while it destroys you.

But when we repent of sin, something wonderful happens. Happiness bursts forth. Joy erupts. Comfort envelops us. Jesus said, *"Blessed* [how happy] *are those who mourn, for they shall be comforted"* (Matthew 5:4). Whenever a sinner repents, he opens the door to real happiness and true comfort.

And God didn't intend repentance merely for unbelievers. The Bible instructs Christians to repent, too:

> *If they fall away, to renew them again to repentance, since they crucify again for themselves the Son of God, and put Him to an open shame.* (Hebrews 6:6)

How do we do this? When you and I discover something in our lives that displeases God, the Bible instructs us to cut it off, to remove it from our lives (see Ephesians 4:24-32).

Before the Nazis executed him shortly before the end of World War II, Dietrich Bonhoeffer coined the phrase "cheap grace." In his book *The Cost of Discipleship* he wrote, "Cheap grace is the preaching of forgiveness without requiring repentance. It's the preaching of baptism without church discipline, communion without confession, absolution without personal confession. Cheap grace is grace without discipleship, grace without the cross. It is grace without Jesus Christ."

Are you clinging to some ritual performed as a child for your salvation? Christenings, confirmations, and communion are all great—but have you undergone an inward transformation? And has that inward transformation shown itself in an outward demonstration? That's what God is looking for.

Some students of a rabbi once asked him what they considered a profound question. "Rabbi," they said. "When is the best time for a person to repent?"

"A man must make sure he repents on the last day of his life," he answered.

The students thought about his reply and then said, "Well, rabbi, how can one know when it's the last day of his life?"

The rabbi smiled and replied, "The answer is simple: Repent now."

God tells Abraham, "Do you want to make your mark on the world? When you allow Me to speak in your life, and when you portray My mark upon your life—when you genuinely repent every time you knowingly sin—then you will become a great ambassador for Me."

One Little Peg

When God told Abraham that he and Sarah would have a son, Abraham fell on his face and laughed. "Shall a child be born to a man who is one hundred years old?" he asked. "Shall Sarah, who is ninety years old, bear a child?"

But God wasn't joking. Because of His wonderful sense of humor, He instructed Abraham to name his new son Isaac.

Isaac means "laughter."

Every time that Abraham spoke to Isaac, he would be reminded. In the very act of calling out his son's name, he would remember what had happened.

"Come here, Laughter." And then he'd chuckle himself.

Since God is who He is—gracious and merciful—He didn't forget about Ishmael. *And as for Ishmael,* God told Abraham, *"I have heard you. Behold, I have blessed him, and will make him fruitful, and will multiply him exceedingly. He shall beget twelve princes, and I will make him a great nation"* (Genesis 17:20). But God would not change His mind about establishing his covenant with Abraham through Isaac.

Although Abraham wanted God to fulfill His promise through Ishmael, God had different plans. He wanted Abraham to go further—to see beyond his flesh, to grasp the massive nature of this divine promise. And He wants us to do the same thing. The lesson for Abraham remains the same for you and me: when God is preparing a future for you, don't cling to the past.

Ishmael represented the past; Isaac symbolized the future. Ishmael represented the flesh; Isaac symbolized the spirit. While Ishmael brought dissension into Abraham's home, Isaac brought laughter.

Do you have an Ishmael in your life? Does it feel too hard to let go of that thing in your past? Instead of praying, "Oh, that Ishmael might live before you," pray, "Oh, that Ishmael might die within me—so that you can bring forth Isaac."

Let it go! God wants to expand your life. Give up holding on to the past.

One final thing: Did you notice that although Abram and Sarai received new names, Ishmael did not? Do you know why God didn't give the young man a new name? It's because Ishmael represented the flesh, and the flesh resists all change. Jesus Christ said, *"That which is born of the flesh is flesh"* (John 3:6). So Ishmael remained Ishmael.

Don't try giving your flesh a new name; don't bother trying to reform it. Kill it. And since we can't change the flesh, we'd better learn how to live in the Spirit. Otherwise, life will be mighty unpleasant for us.

A Haitian wanted to sell his home. Asking price? Two thousand dollars (remember, it's Haiti). A man heard about the home and offered the seller half of that amount because he couldn't afford the asking price.

"I'll sell it to you for half with one stipulation," the owner said. "I will retain ownership of a single nail, protruding from above the front door." The happy buyer was only too eager to strike a deal.

After many years, the original owner returned and wanted to buy back his former house. "No way," said the resident. "My family's here now. We've made our lives here. I have no interest in selling."

The former owner didn't argue and left silently. He found the carcass of a dead dog and hung it from the nail he still owned. Within a week, the family had to sell the house back to the original owner. They couldn't stand the stench; and so the man who owned the nail got his old house back.

What's the moral? If you allow Satan to have just one little peg in your life, he'll hang all of his garbage on it. If you don't deal with what God wants you to deal with, it'll come back to haunt you.

Kill the Spider

For just a few moments, examine your life. Ask yourself:

- Is my spiritual life one of excellence?
- Is it pretty mediocre?
- Am I living just to get by?
- Am I living to please God in everything?

Perhaps you're more like the naval ensign who left his captain behind. You're charging through life. You've made plans. You're traveling at breakneck speed. The only problem is—God's not aboard. You need the Captain to speak truth into your life, to mark your life with obvious transformation, and to expand your life in new horizons.

A certain deacon attended his church's prayer meeting every Wednesday night. Week after week, he repeated the same prayer: "And Lord, clear out all those cobwebs in my life." (By "cobwebs" he meant all the things that marred his testimony.)

The prayer meetings came and went, but the deacon's prayer never changed: "And Lord, clear out all those cobwebs in my life."

The pattern continued for months, until one regular attendee couldn't take it anymore. At the next prayer meeting when the deacon said, "And Lord, clear out all those cobwebs in my life," the other man yelled, "Don't do it, Lord! Kill the spider!"[4]

If you want to make a mark on your world, then you have to learn to "kill the spider." Repentance of sin—not just confessing it, but turning from it through faith by the power of the Spirit—is a prerequisite to making your mark.

I think Wilbur Chapman had it exactly right: "My life is governed by a single rule. Anything that dims my vision of Christ, anything that takes away my taste for Bible study, anything that cramps my prayer life or makes Christian work difficult is wrong for me; and I must, as a Christian, turn away from it."

Making your mark on the world requires that you pay attention to some key prerequisites. And once you do— you're on your way. His way.

MEDITATING ON THE MARK

In this chapter we learned that before Abraham could make his mark for God, God had to make His own mark in the life of Abraham. Before you can go forward with your Godprint, there are three prerequisites: permit God to speak, portray His mark, and prepare for Him to expand your life.

Permit. Sometimes when God speaks into our lives we don't like what He has to say. What clever barriers do you use to keep God out? Which passages in Scripture do you avoid reading because the Word is "sharper" than a two-edged sword?

Portray. Abraham's outward action, the circumcision as a symbol of God's covenant with Israel, was symbolic of Abraham's faith in God and repentance toward Him. Has your inward transformation resulted in an outward demonstration of repentance?

Prepare. When God works to prepare a future for you, do not cling to your past. What percentage of your life would you say that you truly allow God to completely control? Who or what controls the other percentage?

MODELING THE MASTER'S MARK

Permit. 2 Timothy 3:16-17: *"All Scripture is given by inspiration of God, and is profitable for doctrine, for reproof, for correction, for instruction in righteousness, that the man of God may be complete, thoroughly equipped for every good work."*

Portray. Romans 2:4: *"Or do you despise the riches of His goodness, forbearance, and longsuffering, not knowing that the goodness of God leads you to repentance?"*

Prepare. Psalm 2:12: *"Blessed are all those who put their trust in Him."*

MAKING YOUR MARK

In the Book of 1 Chronicles, Jabez prays that God *"would bless me indeed, and enlarge my territory"* (1 Chronicles 4:10). Make a list in your prayer journal of what God has already blessed you with, and ask Him for very specific blessings in the week to come.

CHAPTER TEN

How to Be God's Friend

An oxymoron is a self-contradiction, a combination of contradictory or incongruous words. Consider a few examples from a list called "Top Oxymorons":

Legally drunk
Exact estimate
Resident alien
Clearly misunderstood
Peace force
Political science
Microsoft Works [1]

I wonder about the last one, though. Shouldn't the top oxymoron really be "God's friend"? After all, to claim friendship necessitates a mutuality, a commonality. Friendship puts two individuals on the same level. And how could a holy, perfect God ever call a flawed human being His friend?

That's exactly what He did with Abraham. (See 2 Chronicles 20:7; Isaiah 41:8; James 2:23.)

God is infinitely above everyone and everything else, but three times Scripture calls Abraham God's friend. God takes Abraham from way down in the pit and lifts him up with the highest honor: "You're my Friend."

And while the thought of being God's friend boggles our minds, it definitely delights our hearts. We smile when we read the words of Jesus to His disciples:

> *No longer do I call you servants, for a servant does not know what his master is doing; but I have called you friends, for all things that I heard from My Father I have made known to you.* (John 15:15)

In fact, if you have God as your Friend, you don't need much else. I'd rather have God as my Friend and the whole world as my enemy than to have all the friends in the world and have God as my enemy.

What does it mean to be God's friend? We know that God loves us and cares for us. But what are the requirements for becoming God's friend? Let's look at Abraham's life and see how he became the friend of God.

Out of Nowhere

One day, as Abraham sat at the door of his tent in the hot afternoon, something unexpected happened. When he looked up, *"Behold, three men were standing by him"* (Genesis 18:2). Abraham looked out across the landscape, nothing but the same scenery, when suddenly—behold!—three men showed up. Unannounced and totally unexpected.

Clearly, these weren't three ordinary men. The Scripture says, *"Then the LORD appeared to him* [Abraham]" (Genesis 18:1).

What would you do? What if Jesus just showed up at your front door, in the flesh, unannounced, and out of the blue? For Abraham and Sarah, it meant they had no time to vacuum the tent, clean up Ishmael's dirty socks, or wash Abraham's breakfast dishes.

Who were these three men? Some commentators see them as a picture of the Trinity, because a few times in this passage we see the three individuals referred to as a single person. In fact, to this day, the Church of England reads Genesis 18 on what it calls Trinity Sunday.

I think it's better to understand these three "men" as two angels tagging along with God—a theophany. Or as some people think, a Christophany—an incarnation of Christ in the Old Testament. For example, when the visit with Abraham ends we read, *"Then the men turned away from there and went toward Sodom, but Abraham still stood before the LORD"* (Genesis 18:22). Immediately after that we read, *"Now the two angels came to Sodom in the evening"* (Genesis 19:1). When you put all the Scriptures together, you get the idea that the Lord came to see Abraham—accompanied by two angels.

Remember, the New Testament verse tells us: *"Do not forget to entertain strangers, for by so doing some have unwittingly entertained angels"* (Hebrews 13:2). Abraham entertained angels! But far more importantly, he played host to God himself. Suddenly, spontaneously, the trio simply showed up, unannounced—and Abraham welcomed their visit.

Good friendships withstand spontaneity. Sometimes friends just show up. They don't call or say they're coming; they just appear at your door. Jesus remarked on this kind of spontaneity when He said, *"Which of you shall have a friend, and go to him at midnight and say to him, 'Friend, lend me three loaves'"* (Luke 11:5).

If you're God's friend, get used to spontaneity. God shows up and works in your life whenever He wants to. We can't predict His visitation or His testing. He rarely warns us before He gets our attention; He just shows up and grabs it. We sit there with our feet up, relaxing, and enjoying the day—and then we get a phone call that changes our future.

And it could be God who's doing it.

Isaac Newton's first law of motion states, "Everything continues in a state of rest unless it is compelled to change for forces impressed upon it." I think his statement should also be called the first law of friendship with God. God can—and does—barge into our lives whenever He wants to. A beatitude we don't find in Scripture still gives us a good reminder: "Blessed are the flexible, for they shall not be broken."

In a friendship with God, you have to get used to His spontaneity. He shows up whenever He wants to, to do whatever He wants to, however He wants to do it. To be God's friend means to be open and willing to change. We have to refuse to get in a rut. We have to expect God to do the unexpected.

A man bought a radio, took it home, and tuned it to WSM, the home of the "Grand Ole Opry." He pulled off all the knobs and threw them away. Then he took the radio and placed it on top of the refrigerator so nobody could reach it. All he ever wanted to hear was on that one station.

But we can't do that with God. We can't tune in to one frequency and expect that things will never change, because God has editing rights over our lives. He does as He pleases, when He pleases, how He pleases.

> *He does according to His will in the army of heaven and among the inhabitants of the earth. No one can restrain His hand or say to Him, "What have You done?"* (Daniel 4:35)

In Abraham's case, the Lord simply appeared—as if out of nowhere. He specializes in the unexpected visit, the unannounced call.

If you're His friend, He'll do the same with you. So learn to value spontaneity in your walk with God. Become His friend.

Audience of One

When Abraham saw the unusual trio coming toward him, he ran from his tent door and bowed to the ground. Did he recognize one of the men as the Lord? The Bible doesn't tell us. So perhaps Abram simply did what many people from ancient Middle Eastern cultures did when a visitor arrived. He bowed.

But imagine the scene: here was a ninety-nine-year-old man, bowing himself to the ground. In ancient Persia, those who greeted royalty customarily fell to their knees and then gradually inclined forward until their forehead touched the ground. It was a sign of deep humility.

From his prostrated position, Abraham said, *"My Lord, if I have now found favor in Your sight, do not pass on by Your servant"* (Genesis 18:3). The word "Lord" here translates to the Hebrew term *adonai*, the name that servants used to address their masters. The Old Testament often uses the term to describe people rendering humble worship to God.

Notice that Abraham, the ninety-nine-year-old patriarch, referred to himself as a "servant." Remember that Abraham was wealthy now and his neighbors revered him as an international statesman. In the Middle East today, his exalted status would probably earn him the title of sheikh. But Abraham didn't flaunt his wealth—he was very humble before this mysterious trio. He recognized, "I'm not the great sheikh. I'm your servant." And so he bowed low.

One minister loved to tell how he had he survived the Johnstown Flood. He made sure that everybody he met understood this part of his personal history. He told and retold his story every chance he had—something like, "Can you top this one?" As the years passed, this guy grew old, died, and went to Heaven. When testimony time came, the old preacher walked up to Peter and said, "Can I share tonight my testimony of how I survived the Johnstown Flood? It's a great story; everyone will love it."

"Sure," Peter said, "but remember—Noah is in the audience tonight."

Whenever we begin to paint ourselves in a flattering light, we need to remember that God is in our audience. In fact, God is our audience.

Abraham—this great, venerable, wealthy sheikh, with 318 servants at his beck and call—bows down and worships his Lord. He shows us that worship is the proper response to divine friendship. When we count God as our Friend, worship should flow naturally from our lives. Humble worship is one of the most selfless acts possible. In true worship, we take all of the focus off of ourselves and place it squarely on God. That's why we need to be careful about saying things like, "I don't like that music; it's too loud. It's too hard. It's too fast. It's too slow. It's too contemporary. It's too old. It's too … whatever." Who cares? Genuine worship is a humble response to a divine friendship in which the focus—every bit of it—remains on God alone. The psalmist wrote, *"Oh come, let us worship and bow down; let us kneel before the Lord our Maker"* (Psalm 95:6).

Approaching God in humility requires two things. First, we must see God as He really is; second, we must see ourselves as we truly are. When we see God for who He really is and we see ourselves as we really are, worship happens naturally. And if it doesn't happen, then something has gone wrong. Either we're not seeing who we really are, or we're not seeing God as He really is.

When the prophet Isaiah had a majestic vision of God, *"sitting on a throne, high and lifted up,"* he could say nothing but *"Woe is me, for I am undone! Because I am a man of unclean lips, and I dwell in the midst of a people of unclean lips"* (Isaiah 6:1; 5). Now why did Isaiah react like this? He had an astonishing experience that very few people have ever had. Had he lived today, he could have gone on a speaking tour: "I Saw God." Certainly he'd make the rounds on Christian television. Then he'd sell millions of books. Because he saw who God really was, he became acutely aware of who he really was. And a deep conviction came upon him that naturally brought forth humble worship.

Show me someone filled with pride and I will show you someone who can't count God as his Friend. *"God resists the proud, but gives grace to the humble,"* declares Scripture (James 4:6; 1 Peter 5:5). If God is your Friend—if you see Him as He really is and you recognize yourself as you really are—then you'll respond to your divine Friend with humility and worship.

"You don't impress the officials at NASA with a paper airplane," someone once said.[2] It makes sense, doesn't it? You don't brag about your crayon sketches in the presence of Picasso. You don't claim equality with Einstein because you can write the formula H^2O. And you don't get all excited about your own goodness when you stand in the presence of the perfect One.

If you count God as your Friend, then humility marks your divine friendship. It also marks your dealings with the men and women made in His image. Humility and friendship with God go hand-in-hand.

God's Cow

I find it remarkable that this ninety-nine-year-old man served three mysterious guests in the heat of a summer day. And he invited them into his tent.

In salvation, God comes only by invitation; He never forces His way into a life. Jesus said, *"Behold, I stand at the door and knock. If anyone hears My voice and opens the door, I will come in to him and dine with him, and he with Me"* (Revelation 3:20). Jesus won't come in unless you invite Him in.

Abraham invited the men into his home and immediately set about to serve them. *"My Lord,"* he said, *"if I have now found favor in Your sight, do not pass on by Your servant. Please let a little water be brought, and wash your feet, and rest yourselves under the tree. And I will bring a morsel of bread, that you may refresh your hearts. After that you may pass by, inasmuch as you have come to your servant."* And the trio said in unison: *"Do as you have said."* (Genesis 18:3-5)

Abraham hurried inside and spoke to Sarah, *"Quickly, make ready three measures of fine meal; knead it and make cakes"* (Genesis 18:6). Abraham ran to the herd, took a good and tender calf, and instructed a young servant to prepare it quickly. Finally he took butter and milk and the quickly prepared calf and set it before the men. Then he stood by them under the shade of a tree until they had finished eating.

Abraham served his guests personally. Certainly he involved Sarah and his servants, but he placed himself squarely in the center of this service. He was a ninety-nine-year-old wealthy sheikh who easily could have folded his arms and barked out orders to any one of his 318 servants. But he didn't. He served personally—he "ran," he "hurried," he "hastened," he "prepared," he "set" food before his guests, and he "stood" by as they sat to eat.

At first, I doubt that Abraham understood who had come to visit him. I don't think he told Sarah, "Uh, honey? God's here with a couple of His angels. So let's have a nice meal." Nevertheless, he got involved personally; he didn't pass the buck to his servants with the excuse, "Well, that's what I pay them to do."

If you want to be a friend of God, you need to carry out some kind of ministry. You must serve God in some capacity—every Christian has a ministry. In fact, a Christian without a ministry is a contradiction. There comes a point when it's not enough to pat your pastor on the head, give him a check, and say, "Now go do it. That's why we pay you." There's a place for tithing, of course, but all of us need to serve the Lord in a personal way.

And regardless of how we serve, let's remember that all ministries are to the Lord first. Before Old Testament priests served the congregation, God told them, "You will serve Me by doing this for them." The servants of the Lord first ministered to the Lord. Yes, they offered sacrifices for the people and brought them the Word; but their first responsibility was to the Lord.

So much of ministry happens in secret. Nobody knows about it. No one applauds or offers encouragement, because no one sees what's happening behind the scenes—and that can make certain ministries feel unappreciated. But if we're serving the Lord first—"I'm doing this as unto the Lord. This is hard for me, but it's for you, Lord"—it makes all the difference. Jesus said, *"Inasmuch as you did it to one of the least of these My brethren, you did it to Me"* (Matthew 25:40).

In the poem "I Wonder," Ruth Harms Caukin wrote, "You know, Lord, how I serve you with great emotional fervor in the limelight. You know how eagerly I speak for you at a women's club. You know how genuine my enthusiasm is at a Bible study. But how would I react, I wonder, if you pointed to a basin of water and asked me to wash the calloused feet of a bent and wrinkled old woman, day after day, month after month, in a room where nobody saw and nobody knew?"

Abraham served his Friend because he loved Him. He served with eagerness. He served immediately. Once more, remember that he's ninety-nine, it's a hot day, but he was out there running around. Only when he finished his ministry to the Lord did he stand still—and even then he stood under a tree while his guests sat and ate.

If Abraham based his service on his feelings, he probably never would've served at all. He could have offered a lot of excuses: "I'm old. It's hot. I have a headache. I'm tired. I have 318 servants to do that kind of stuff." But he served immediately, perhaps thinking, *This is who I am—this what I'm going to do—whether I feel like it or not.*

Someone once said, "The greatest ability is dependability."[3] Give me somebody who's dependable, someone who has said in her heart, "I'm going to serve," rather than anyone famous. Any day.

Abraham also served generously. He gave everything he had. Sarah baked bread from fine meal, while the meat came from a tender and good calf.

Serving God should cost us something. When David wanted a threshing floor to build a temple, he approached the owner to buy it. The man said, "If you want it, I'll give it to you." But David replied, *"No, but I will surely buy it from you for a price; nor will I offer burnt offerings to the LORD my God with that which costs me nothing"* (2 Samuel 24:24). Don't give God leftovers, whether it's leftover time or leftover resources. Give God the best you have. In the Old Testament, God told His people to give Him the best from the flock, the best from the grain, the best that they had. And by giving their best stuff to God, they proved that their best stuff was not their god.

A farmer had two cows. "One's God's and one's mine," he said. But he never identified which was whose. One evening when one of the cows got sick, he went out to the barn to check on it. A few minutes later he came into the house and said to his wife, "Honey, I've got bad news. God's cow just died."

Do you know anyone who does something similar? "These toys are old and used; let's give them to the church." "That piano, it's a piece of junk; I'll bet the church could use it." They give God the dead cow instead of the healthy one.

One day a dollar bill met a twenty-dollar bill. They had known each other for some time, but hadn't seen one another for ages. The dollar bill said to the twenty, "Where've you been? I haven't seen you in awhile."

"I've been around the world," the twenty answered. "I've been on cruise boats, I've been in casinos, and I've been in malls. I've been a lot of different places. Where have you been?"

"Oh, you know," replied the dollar bill. "Same old stuff: church, church, church."

John Henry Jowett once said, "Service that costs nothing accomplishes nothing."

All of It

After the men finished their meal, they asked Abraham, *"Where is Sarah your wife?"* When Abraham told them she was in another part of the tent, the Lord said, *"I will certainly return to you according to the time of life, and behold, Sarah your wife shall have a son"* (Genesis 18:9-10).

Unknown to Abraham, Sarah stood listening to the conversation on the other side of a tent flap. She had passed the time for bearing children many years before, so as she heard this astonishing promise, she *"laughed within herself."* She didn't laugh out loud; she didn't roll on the floor, holding her sides. Abraham didn't hear her, but the Lord did.

> *And the* LORD *said to Abraham, "Why did Sarah laugh, saying, 'Shall I surely bear a child, since I am old?' Is anything too hard for the* LORD? *At the appointed time I will return to you, according to the time of life, and Sarah shall have a son."* (Genesis 18:13-14)

Then Sarah appeared from behind the tent flap and denied it. *"I did not laugh,"* she insisted (see Genesis 18:15). *"And* [the LORD] *said, 'No, but you did laugh!'"* (Genesis 18:15).

Friends trust each other and remain loyal to one another. Three times the Bible calls Abraham the friend of God. Why? Because Abraham trusted God. But Sarah seemed to have trouble trusting God and remaining loyal to Him, despite the staggering promises He made to this couple. Or maybe because the promises seemed so unbelievable.

Although Sarah laughed inwardly, God rebuked her publicly. Not long before, Abraham also laughed at the same promise—but he laughed right out loud. Why did God rebuke Sarah, but not Abraham? Laughter comes in different forms; not all of it is lighthearted. One can laugh cynically, scornfully, arrogantly, even unbelievingly. But when Abraham laughed, he seemed to have done so joyfully—the promise just tickled his funny bone. To think that he and Sarah would become parents at such an old age! Sarah didn't laugh with joy, however; her laugh was more like, "Yeah, right. Like that's ever going to happen."

I remember watching a television interview with a girl who performed some heroic act. As she told the story, she laughed, because it brought her such joy. She didn't laugh because she couldn't believe she acted so heroically, but because she found great joy in looking back on what she did and realizing what it had accomplished.

When God is your Friend, you trust Him and conform to His will. When God is your Friend, you gladly believe His promises and bank on what He says. And you obey Him. Jesus not only said to His disciples, "I don't call you servants, I call you friends," but He also said, *"You are My friends if you do whatever I command you"* (John 15:14). We show our friendship to Christ by obeying Him in all things, not just in some things. You can't call God your Friend and then try to pick and choose in which areas of your life you'll obey Him. He wants a total conformity to His will.

Friends of God don't say, "I'll obey Him in my business, but not in my marriage."

They don't say, "I'll obey Him in my marriage, but not on my income taxes."

They don't say, "I'll obey Him in my work, but not in my leisure time."

Friends of God express a consistent conformity to His will. God wants it all.

Friends Forever

On their fortieth wedding anniversary, a husband and wife got a visit from a fairy. Both were sixty years old.

"Because you two have been such a good, loving couple for so many years, I'm going to grant each of you one wish," the fairy said.

Without hesitation, the wife said, "I know what I want. I want to travel the world!" So the fairy waved her magic wand and, Poof! The wife had tickets in her hand to travel anywhere on Earth.

"Now it's your turn," said the fairy to the husband. "You get one wish, too. What do you want?"

He thought for a moment, looked at his wife, looked down, and then said softly, "Well, I'd like to have a wife who's thirty years younger than I am."

"No problem," said the fairy. She waved her wand and, Poof! Instantly, the man was ninety years old.

Aren't you glad that God doesn't deal with us according to our foolishness? God rebuked Sarah for laughing, but in a gracious and mild way. He didn't lay into her or pronounce a curse on her or age her by thirty years. He insisted that she really did laugh, but then He asked her a question that went straight to the heart of the matter: *"Is anything too hard for the LORD?"*

When we face difficult circumstances, we need to remember God's question—and the obvious answer to it. Nothing is too hard for the Lord.

God doesn't ask if anything is too hard for us; that's a given. All kinds of "too hard for me" things march into our lives and steamroll us in an instant. But none of the things that overtax our abilities present the slightest challenge to the Lord.

Is the "too hard" thing in your life something in your family? Your spouse? Your children? Your parents? Is it something in your business or with one of your friends? No matter what, remember that nothing is too hard for God.

So if you have a huge burden that you know you can give to your trustworthy and almighty Friend, why not give it to Him? *"Is anything too hard for the LORD?"* Our problems—despite their overwhelming size to us—do not challenge Him in the least.

Nothing is impossible for God.

Some years ago a writer imagined that Jesus wrote a note to one of His children. Maybe the Lord wrote it to you:

I had to write and tell you how much I love and care for you. Yesterday I saw you walking and laughing with your friends. I hope that soon you'd want Me to walk along with you, too, so I painted you a sunset to close your day and whispered a cool breeze to refresh you. I waited; you never called. I just kept on loving you, though.

As I watched you, I wanted to touch you. I spilled moonlight on your face, trickling down your cheeks as so many tears have. I wanted so much to comfort you. The next day I exploded a brilliant sunrise into the glorious morning for you. But you woke up late and rushed off to work; you didn't notice. My sky became cloudy; My tears were in the rain. I really do love you.

I try to say it in the quiet of the green meadow and in the blue sky. The wind whispers My love throughout the treetops and spills into the vibrant colors of all the flowers. I shouted to you in the thunder of the great waterfalls and composed love songs for birds to sing to you. I warm you with My sunshine and perfume the air with nature's sweet scent. My love for you is deeper than any ocean and greater than any need in your heart. If you'd only realize how much I care!

My Father sends His love. I want you to meet Him; He cares, too. Fathers are just that way. So please call on Me, soon. No matter how long it takes, I'll wait, because I love you.

Your Friend,

Jesus[3]

Has your Friend been trying to get your attention? He wants to hear from you. Jesus loves when you commit and trust everything to Him—nothing is too hard for Him.

The music director of a church in Ohio passed by his Sunday school department and overheard an eight-year-old boy praying publicly for his class. As the man listened, he wrote down the prayer. "Dear God," it began, "bless our fathers and bless our mothers and bless our teachers and bless our sisters and bless our brothers. And God, please take care of yourself, because if anything happens to you, we're all sunk."[4]

He was right. If anything did happen to God, we would all be sunk. For Abraham, that would have meant no Promised Land, no promised son, no covenant. And for us it would mean no resurrection, no hope, and no eternal life.

But since God is our eternal, unchanging, loving Friend, we have nothing to worry about. He's not going anywhere. One day, however, we'll go to be with Him. After all, friends belong together.

And in this case, forever.

MEDITATING ON THE MARK

In this chapter we learned that Abraham is called God's friend three times in Scripture. There are four components that will help you to become a friend of God: spontaneity, humility, ministry, and conformity.

Spontaneity. Good friendships withstand spontaneity. When have your "plans" gone awry because God has stepped in?

Humility. Remember that God is always your first audience. When was the last time that you physically bowed down in prayer and worship before Him?

Ministry. A Christian without a ministry is a contradiction. In what way are you personally serving the Lord?

Conformity. In one sense, Sarah had a problem with loyalty, trust, and obedience in the Lord. In which area(s) of your life are you picking and choosing whether or not Christ is in complete control?

MODELING THE MASTER'S MARK

Spontaneity. Proverbs 14:12: *"There is a way that seems right to a man, but its end is the way of death."*

Humility. Psalm 95:6: *"Oh come, let us worship and bow down; let us kneel before the* LORD *our Maker."*

Ministry. Colossians 4:17: *"Take heed to the ministry which you have received in the Lord, that you may fulfill it."*

Conformity. 2 Corinthians 10:5: *"Bringing every thought into captivity to the obedience of Christ."*

MAKING YOUR MARK

In Genesis 18:14, we are asked the question: "Is anything too hard for the LORD?" Make a list of three things in your life right now that are just too hard for you to deal with. Are they too hard for the Lord?

CHAPTER ELEVEN

Have I Got Plans for You!

On the first day, God created the cow. "You must go to the field with the farmer all day long and suffer under the sun and have calves and give milk to support the farmer," God said. "I will give you a lifespan of sixty years."

"That's kind of a tough life you want me to live for sixty years," the cow replied. "Let me have twenty years and I'll give you back the other forty." God agreed.

On the second day, God created the dog. "Sit all day by the door of your house and bark at anyone who comes in or walks past," God said. "I will give you a lifespan of twenty years."

"That's too long to be barking," the dog answered. "Give me ten years and I'll give you back the other ten." So God agreed.

On the third day, God created the monkey and said, "Entertain people, do monkey tricks, make them laugh. I'll give you a twenty-year lifespan."

"How boring," said the monkey. "Tricks for twenty years? I don't know; the dog gave you back ten, so that's what I'll do. Is that okay?" And God agreed.

On the fourth day, God created man. "Eat, sleep, play, enjoy, do nothing, just enjoy, enjoy," God said. "I'll give you twenty years."

"What?" answered man. "Only twenty years? No way! I'll tell you what. I'll take my twenty and the forty the cow gave back, and the ten the dog gave back, and the ten the monkey gave back; that makes eighty. Okay?"

"Okay," God said, "you've got a deal."

So that is why for the first twenty years we eat, sleep, play, enjoy, and do nothing. For the next forty years we slave in the sun to support our family. For the next ten years we do monkey tricks to entertain our grandchildren, and for the last ten years we sit in the front of the house and bark at everybody.[1]

Welcome to life.

Of course, God has a greater plan for our lives than that. Much greater!

Whatever plans our parents had for us, whatever plans we've made for ourselves, we need to stop and ask, "What is God's plan? What does He want?" If you're a believer in Christ, recognize that God purchased your life at a great price. Paul said, *"You are not your own"* (1 Corinthians 6:19). Now to discover God's plan for you.

Life is no accident. You're not a fortuitous concourse of meaningless protoplasm. Your life has purpose, a plan. Paul said, *"Therefore do not be unwise, but understand what the will of the Lord is"* (Ephesians 5:17).

Have you ever watched the movie *Chariots of Fire*? In one scene Eric Liddell, the Olympic athlete, made a decision on what to do with his life. He wanted to run in the Olympics, but he also felt God tugging his heart toward China. He and his sister, Jenny, stood on a hillside overlooking a Scottish city. "Jenny," he said. "I know God made me for a purpose. For China. But he also made me fast. And when I run, I feel His pleasure." I love that sentence, because it gives such focus to God's purpose and plan for Liddell's life.

The second half of Genesis 18 focuses on the overarching theme of God's purpose and plan for Abraham's life. It introduces three primary spheres: public, private, and prayer. As you ponder Abraham's experience, ponder your own. Keep asking yourself, *What is God's purpose and plan* for me?

A Public Plan for Abraham

God called Abraham to be an instrument of divine blessing—that was part of His plan for Abraham's life. And so God included Abraham in issues that involved God's dealings with the wider world.

God asks an interesting question:

> *And the LORD said, "Shall I hide from Abraham*
> *what I am doing, since Abraham shall surely become*
> *a great and mighty nation, and all the nations of the*
> *earth shall be blessed in him?"* (Genesis 18:17-18)

The Lord's question leads me to ask a question of my own: To whom is God speaking? Is He talking to himself? My dad used to say, "I like to talk to myself—because I like to hear a wise man talk and I like to talk to a wise man." So is this some kind of inter-Trinitarian communication? Is God simply speaking out loud in the presence of two angels? Or is He rhetorically asking the question in Abraham's hearing?

He's speaking out loud. We know the two angels who accompanied God on this visit haven't yet left. And Abraham is with them. What we know for sure is that after God speaks, Abraham responds—indicating Abraham's public purpose.

God promised Abraham that he would become a great nation. His family grew from just himself and Sarah; to Abraham, Sarah, and Ishmael; to Abraham, Sarah, Ishmael, and Isaac; to a tribal group; and eventually to an entire nation. Today, every Jew and all Arabs—millions and millions of people—trace their lineage to father Abraham.

The nation of Israel is an amazing land made up of an amazing group of people. I've visited Israel twenty-six times. In my early twenties, I lived there in a kibbutz. God has uniquely blessed the Jews. The Jewish population comprises just one-tenth of 1 percent of the world population, and yet Jews have received 33 percent of all Nobel Peace prizes and hold 30 percent of all awards in music, science, and literature. Albert Einstein is one of their most influential representatives. They have contributed greatly to the world's welfare in many areas. Consider some examples from the world of medicine: the Wasserman test for syphilis; digitalis (discovered by Dr. Newslan); chlorohydrate to treat convulsions (discovered by Dr. Liffreich); streptomycin (discovered by Dr. Abraham Waxman); a polio pill by Dr. Albert Sabin; the polio vaccine by Jonas Salk. A blessed group of people! And the world has been blessed through them.

But it's also a miraculous nation. The nation of Israel has survived hardships unlike any other nation. After four hundred years of slavery, two deportations, almost two thousand years of dispersal around the world, an Inquisition, and the Holocaust, the Jewish people continue to exist—and even to thrive. Jerusalem has suffered thirty-six wars, seventeen times she's been leveled to the ground, and eighteen times she's risen up from the ashes. Why?

God made a covenant with Abraham, didn't He? And He said very clearly to Israel:

> *The LORD did not set His love on you nor choose you because you were more in number than any other people, for you were the least of all peoples;*

but because the LORD *loves you....* " (Deuteronomy 7:7-8a)

That statement interests me. Because, in essence, God said, "Do you know why I love you? I love you because I love you—and that's all the reason I need. It's not because of you or because of anything you've done. It's because of Me and My greatness that I love you."

Parents can relate to this. Sometimes they look at a face that only a mother could love. I know that at the times I disappointed my parents, my mother always stood by me to shower me with love (as well as to discipline me). The great nation of Israel arose so Abraham could say, "God made me for a purpose." God planned to bless the world through Abraham.

You might think, *Well, that's great for Abraham. Congratulations, Abe, you're a great guy! But what does that have to do with me? Chances are, I'm not going to become a great nation.* Maybe not in the same way as Abraham, but a nation is simply the expansion of one person's life to great proportions. And I think God wants to do that with each of us.

We should all stop every so often and ask ourselves, *What's my purpose? Why am I here on this Earth? Am I here merely to make a comfortable living? Just to breathe air for seventy or eighty years and wear nice clothes and then die? Is that my purpose?* Not according to God, it's not.

Do you know God's purpose for your life? A lot of people never get an answer to that question. They don't think, *What's the great purpose for my life publicly?* Instead, they wonder, *What about me? What about my needs?* Someone well said that a person all wrapped up in himself makes a very small package.

Abraham had a divine purpose: not to live a self-centered life, but to bless others.

As the Lord, the two angels, and Abraham stood on a ridge overlooking the Dead Sea and down on the cities of the plain, only Abraham had no idea of the cataclysmic events about to occur.

The Dead Sea is unique. First, it's the lowest spot on Earth—1,290 feet below sea level. Second, it has no outlet. Plenty of water comes in every day—from the Jordan River in the north, from the Arnon River on the east, from the Kidron River on the west—but it doesn't let out any water. Many inlets, plus no outlet, equal a Dead Sea. Obviously, the Dead Sea supports no organic life (hence the name "Dead" Sea). There aren't any fishermen.

The same principle holds true in human lives. Many inlets and no outlet make for a very dead person. When someone organizes life totally around what he or she can get, but not what he or she can give, you get a human Dead Sea.

God uniquely blessed Abraham. He gave him wealth, hundreds of servants, and eventually mobs of grandkids and great-grandkids. But he was no Dead Sea. Everything that came into his life also flowed out of his life.

Maybe you've been floundering. You've lived as though the whole world owes you something—and you feel like the Dead Sea. How about adopting a new strategy? Ask, "How can I become a blessing to others?" instead of, "How can others bless me?" Change your focus. Stop the myopia. Look around and see what you can do for others.

Someone asked the famous psychiatrist Dr. Karl Menninger, "What would you do if you knew you were about to have a nervous breakdown?" He answered, "I'd go and find someone in worse condition than myself and try and help him." He knew health flows from taking the focus off of oneself and placing it on others. It's a sure cure.

A suicidal young man named Eddie found truth in Dr. Menninger's prescription. Life took some turns he didn't expect; in fact, it moved in the opposite direction he desired. So he decided to end his life by jumping off a bridge into a river below. A stranger named Jim saw him jump and leaped into the water to save Eddie. Unfortunately, Jim didn't know how to swim. Eddie could swim, and when he saw Jim struggling, he knew that he was going to drown. Something inside Eddie stirred and he swam toward the stranger who came to save him; and Eddie, the suicidal guy, saved Jim. From that moment on, his entire focus changed. The opportunity to bless someone else brought him a sense of hope and meaning—it changed his life.

We tend to get immersed in our own troubles and woes. We look inwardly when we should be looking outwardly. God planned for Abraham to bless the world, which gave Abraham a public focus. That same focus makes up part of God's plan for us.

God intended to use Abraham as the instrument through which the Messiah—man's salvation—would eventually come into the world. And everyone who names Jesus Christ as Lord is called to let their light shine among men—to bring the brilliance of Jesus Christ into every dark corner of the world. Jesus said, *"Go into all the world and preach the gospel to every creature"* (Mark 16:15). We have a job to bless the world by bringing the gospel.

In 1963, it took two hours for the world to hear of the assassination of John F. Kennedy. Thirty-six years later, it took just a few minutes for the world to hear of the death of John F. Kennedy, Jr. when his plane went down in the Atlantic.

Now think of this: two thousand years ago, Jesus Christ died on a Cross outside of Jerusalem—and half the world still doesn't know about it. Half the world! God did not plan for the Church to become a "bless me" club where

His people come to get stroked. He has given us a public purpose, so that the message we proclaim will bless all the nations of the world.

A Private Plan for Abraham

God's plan for Abraham also included private service. God said:

> For I have known him, in order that he may command his children and his household after him, that they keep the way of the LORD, to do righteousness and justice, that the LORD may bring to Abraham what He has spoken to him. (Genesis 18:19)

Do you see how God rounded the corner? "Not only are you to influence the world, Abraham, you're also to influence your own family, your own children." How? By "trickle-down righteousness." By Abraham modeling the kind of life God wanted him to live, so that he would influence Ishmael and Isaac and anybody else in his household for good, including the servants. By seeing Abraham model righteousness, they would also want to follow God's commandments and live righteously.

Of course, that doesn't always happen, but in general, children inherit certain propensities of their parents. Your child will spend 16 percent of his or her lifetime in school. One percent will be spent in Sunday school. Eighty-three percent will be spent at home.

It all begins at home.

If parents tolerate evil, then their kids will probably grow up tolerating evil. If parents have foul mouths, their children will probably speak with profanities. If parents are godly, most kids will model their behavior and act in godly ways. I don't mean that your kids will wear halos—you didn't, and neither will they. You might even be dealing with some rebellion right now.

You've given them Scripture. You've tried to model godly behavior, but they're not responding. I guess that means they're becoming adults; they're choosing their own way. Some parents feel tempted to check out at this stage and follow the advice of Mark Twain: "Things run pretty smoothly 'til your kid reaches thirteen. That's the time you need to stick him in a barrel, hammer the lid down nice and snug, and feed him through the knothole. Then, about the time he turns sixteen, plug up the knothole."

Funny. But terrible advice.

Don't check out as a parent—live in such a way that your kids see how your faith guides your conduct. The Lord says to you exactly what He said to Abraham: "I have a plan for you publicly, but I also have a plan for you privately. Live righteously and keep God's commands, so that your kids will want to follow Christ."

Did you notice that while God addressed Abraham on this issue, he did not address Sarah? Sarah certainly had a huge role in the home, but God placed the heaviest responsibility on Abraham: "Abraham, you're running a relay race. You're going to make your lap around the track carrying the baton, but the time will come when you must pass it off to the next generation. And the way you run will speak volumes to Ishmael and to Isaac."

Research has shown that if both Mom and Dad attend church regularly, the odds are 72 percent that their children will remain faithful spiritually. If only Dad attends church and not Mom, their kids have a 55 percent chance of following Christ. If only Mom—and not Dad—goes to church, the odds drop to 15 percent. A father's influence overshadows all of the efforts of Sunday school and public or even private education combined.[2]

Charles Haddon Spurgeon said, "A man's life is always more forcible than his speech. People reckon his deeds as dollars, his words as pennies." The University of New Mexico studied violent crime and drug use among teenagers. They found Albuquerque, where I pastor, has twice the national average. Several factors help to explain the difference, but one of the most prominent is absentee fathers—dads who have abandoned or checked out of the family unit.[3]

God said, "Abraham, don't check out. Don't get so involved in the public ministry of blessing the world that you neglect your own family."

So why is the father so important?

Children usually form their initial ideas of God from how they view their fathers. We call our dads "father," and we address God as "heavenly Father"—and that creates an image. We all approach our relationship with God through a certain grid.

If you have a daughter, she's probably going to marry one day. She's going to look for certain characteristics in a spouse, and she needs to know what to look for. Fathers can help by modeling the right characteristics.

And if you have a son, he'll most likely marry. He needs to know what to become, what to be. Dads should be an example of the necessary traits.

The single most important thing a man can do is love God with all of his mind, heart, soul, and strength—and then to model that kind of relationship in his family. Paul wrote, *"And you, fathers, do not provoke your children to wrath, but bring them up in the training and admonition of the Lord"* (Ephesians 6:4).

It is much easier to build a boy than it is to repair a man—a lesson our culture is having a hard time learning. God says to all of us: "Besides my public plan for you, I have a private one, too."

A Prayerful Plan for Abraham

The ancient cities of Sodom and Gomorrah stood at the southern end of the Dead Sea. Today a bitumen and salt formation covers the whole area; it's part of the great Syro-African rift that runs from Armenia all the way down to central Africa. Experts think that the current Dead Sea area resulted from a catastrophic earthquake that raised the level of the sea and buried Sodom and Gomorrah after a brimstone event. The flammable bitumen in the area remains ignitable to this day.[4]

God moved against these two ancient cities in response to an outcry against them. Who protested? Maybe it was Lot. The New Testament calls Lot a "righteous man" who felt "oppressed" and "tormented" about the wickedness he saw and heard day after day in Sodom (see 2 Peter 2:7). We've seen that Lot was far from perfect—but compared to the residents of Sodom, he was righteous. When he saw and heard the violence and evil there, he cried out to God.

And because He is fair and patient, the Lord dispatched a couple of angels to get a direct appraisal of the situation. God is patient, but never mistake His patience for an inability or unwillingness to act. When Abraham heard that God was about to destroy the cities of the plain, he entered into an extensive prayer session with the Lord:

And Abraham came near and said, "Would You also destroy the righteous with the wicked? Suppose there were fifty righteous within the city; would You also destroy the place and not spare it for the fifty righteous that were in it? Far be it from You to do such a thing as this, to slay the righteous with the wicked, so that the righteous should be as the wicked; far be it from You! Shall not the Judge of all the earth do right?"

> So the LORD said, "If I find in Sodom fifty righteous within the city, then I will spare all the place for their sakes."
>
> Then Abraham answered and said, "Indeed now, I who am but dust and ashes have taken it upon myself to speak to the LORD: Suppose there were five less than fifty righteous; would You destroy all of the city for lack of five?"
>
> So He said, "If I find there forty-five, I will not destroy it."
>
> And he spoke to Him yet again and said, "Suppose there should be forty found there?"
>
> So He said, "I will not do it for the sake of forty."
>
> Then he said, "Let not the Lord be angry, and I will speak: Suppose thirty should be found there?"
>
> So He said, "I will not do it if I find thirty there."
>
> And he said, "Indeed now, I have taken it upon myself to speak to the Lord: Suppose twenty should be found there?"
>
> So He said, "I will not destroy it for the sake of twenty."
>
> Then he said, "Let not the Lord be angry, and I will speak but once more: Suppose ten should be found there?"
>
> And He said, "I will not destroy it for the sake of ten." So the LORD went His way as soon as He had finished speaking with Abraham; and Abraham returned to his place. (Genesis 18:23-33)

Some people read this text and think they're hearing an argument. If you've ever been to Israel and gone to Jerusalem to buy something in the Jewish or the Arab quarter, you've probably bickered back and forth to get the lowest possible price. But there's no argument here. Abraham isn't backing God into a corner. Notice that the Scripture says, *"When*

[God] *had finished speaking with Abraham,*" not, "When Abraham had finished speaking with God" (Genesis 18:33). God initiated the whole exchange. He spoke out loud what He intended to do in order to ignite the interest of Abraham to pray about it. He led Abraham through His reasoning all the way to its conclusion. All along God wanted to show mercy—but he wanted to get Abraham involved.

Paul wrote:

> *I exhort first of all that supplications, prayers, intercessions, and giving of thanks be made for all men, for kings and all who are in authority, that we may lead a quiet and peaceable life.* (1 Timothy 2:1-2)

Abraham stood in the gap; he was concerned about the lives of the residents of Sodom and Gomorrah. In his prayer he tapped into the very character of God.

The wicked owe the righteous a lot. So often God blesses unbelievers simply because believers have prayed. We find several examples in Scripture: God multiplied Laban's flocks for Jacob's sake; Potiphar prospered because Joseph worked for him; God saved a boat on the way to Rome because of Paul's presence; believing spouses sanctify their unbelieving mates. The mere presence of a believer sometimes brings God's blessing on unbelievers.

Jesus said, *"You are the salt of the earth; but if the salt loses its flavor, how shall it be seasoned"* (Matthew 5:13)? If you are a follower of Christ, then you have a divine purpose: to influence the world around you. Thousands of years ago, before refrigerators, people rubbed salt on meat to act as a preservative. It slowed spoilage and preserved the meat. In a similar way, God calls us to act as a safeguard, to be a moral disinfectant—to make a difference in our world.

During the early Church, slaves made up half of the population of the Roman Empire. If you went to any New

Testament church, you would find a number of slaves and slave owners. And while the early Church never raised one picket sign to eradicate slavery—because of its equal treatment of slaves and free people—slavery gradually disappeared as Christianity spread throughout the Roman Empire. That's the influence of salt.

In nineteenth-century England, William Wilberforce and Lord Ashley Shaftsbury stood against slavery in the British Empire. As they protested, working conditions improved in England. And eventually they led the way in abolishing slavery throughout the empire. Strong Christians act as both salt and light:

> *You are the light of the world.... Let your light so shine before men, that they may see your good works and glorify your Father in heaven.* (Matthew 5:14, 16)

When did your presence stop corruption from spreading? When you enter a room, do people say, "Uh-oh, the Jesus freak is here. Let's take this conversation somewhere else"? You are the salt and the light.

An atheist farmer always ridiculed Christians. He placed a letter to the editor in the local newspaper that read: "I plowed on Sunday, I planted on Sunday, I cultivated on Sunday, I hauled in my crops on Sunday, but I never went to church on Sunday. And I harvested more bushels per acre than anyone else, even those who are God-fearing and never miss a church service."

The editor printed the man's letter, but then added his own note: "God doesn't always settle his accounts in October."[5] The editor acted as both salt and light. And God calls us to do the same.

Don't Lose Your Purpose

We live in a world where God calls us to make a difference. People are drowning all around us.

On a dangerous seacoast prone to shipwrecks stood a crude little lifesaving station; it was really nothing more than a hut. But a few devoted members equipped with only one boat kept a constant watch over the sea. With no thought for themselves, they went out day and night, tirelessly searching for the lost. Some of the rescued, along with others in the area, wanted to become associated with the station and give their time, money, and effort to support its work.

Soon the group bought new boats and trained new crews. As the lifesaving station grew, some of its members complained about its crude and poorly equipped building. They suggested that a more comfortable place should be provided as the first refuge of those saved from the sea. So they replaced the emergency cots with beds and put better furniture in the enlarged building.

In no time at all, the lifesaving station became a popular gathering place for its members. They decorated it beautifully, furnished it exquisitely, and because they used it as a sort of club, fewer members expressed interest in going to sea on lifesaving missions. So they hired lifeboat crews to do the work. Yet the lifesaving motif still prevailed in the club's decoration, complete with a symbolic lifeboat in the room where the club held its initiations.

Then a large ship foundered off the coast and the station's hired crews brought in boatloads of cold, wet, and half-drowned people—some dirty, some sick, some with black or yellow skin. Chaos reigned at the beautiful new club, so the property committee immediately built a shower house outside the club where victims of shipwrecks could get cleaned up before coming inside.

At the group's next meeting, a split took place among the membership. Most members wanted to stop the club's lifesaving activities, noting its unpleasant nature and describing it as a hindrance to the social life of the club. Other members insisted upon lifesaving as the organization's primary purpose and pointed out that it still bore the name of a lifesaving station. The first group voted down the minority and told them that if they wanted to save lives, they should begin their own lifesaving station down the coast. So they did.

As the years went by, the new station went through the same changes that occurred in the old; it evolved into a club. So yet another lifesaving station was founded. History continued to repeat itself; and if you were to visit that seacoast today, you would find a number of exclusive clubs along its shore.

Meanwhile, frequent shipwrecks in the dangerous waters take many lives.

What's your purpose? What's your strategy of living for others? Maybe life has closed in around you and every night you hold a pity party. By God's grace, you can change your focus and look around at who needs your help. Because that's God's plan for your life.

MEDITATING ON THE MARK

In this chapter we learned that your life has been purchased at a great price. Whatever plans you, your parents, and/or your spouse may have for your life do not really matter-God's plans do. He demonstrated the purpose and plan for Abraham's life in three distinct ways: publicly, privately, and prayerfully.

Publicly. God revealed to Abraham that he was to publicly be an instrument of God's blessing. God wants your life to be a blessing to others. Whom have you blessed this week? In what specific ways?

Privately. Abraham was commanded to demonstrate the Lord's righteousness to his own family and children. Are you living in such a way that your family clearly sees your love for the Lord and His commandments?

Prayerfully. Abraham tapped into the very character of God in his prayer on behalf of Sodom and Gomorrah: he showed his true love and concern for others. Whom can you lovingly pray for today?

MODELING THE MASTER'S MARK

Publicly. Acts 20:35: *"And remember the words of the Lord Jesus, that He said, 'It is more blessed to give than to receive.'"*

Privately. Matthew 7:24: *"Therefore whoever hears these sayings of Mine, and does them, I will liken him to a wise man who built his house on the rock."*

Prayerfully. Job 16:17: *"And my prayer is pure."*

MAKING YOUR MARK

Half of the world does not know the name of Jesus Christ and has never heard the gospel. You are called to bless the world by bringing the gospel to them. This week, share the gospel with one person who has never heard or has yet to believe.

CHAPTER TWELVE

The Gift of Laughter for Senior Citizens

Way out in the backwoods, a farmer's wife went into labor. The couple lived too far away in the country to get to a hospital, so they fetched the doctor. (That's what they say in the country: "Go fetch the doctor.")

Since the house had no electricity, the doctor asked the father-to-be to hold up a lantern while he delivered the child. Soon the doctor held a baby boy in his arms. The proud new daddy was about to put down the lantern when the doctor said, "Nope. Nope. Keep that lantern up there! I think there's another one." Sure enough, number two came out—a baby girl.

"Now, hold it," the doctor said. "Don't be too quick to put that lantern down, because believe it or not, I think there's another one." And yet another girl was born.

Exhausted by the episode, the man started to put down the lantern. "I don't know how to tell you this," said the doctor, "but there's a fourth child."

By this point the father was totally bewildered. He looked at the lantern and then turned to the doctor. "Doc," he said, "do you think the light's attracting 'em?"[1]

The birth of a child is always a wonderful moment. But what if you're one hundred years old and your wife is in her nineties? What might that be like? That's Abraham and Sarah's story.

> *And the LORD visited Sarah as He had said, and the LORD did for Sarah as He had spoken. For Sarah conceived and bore Abraham a son in his old age, at the set time of which God had spoken to him. And Abraham called the name of his son who was born to him—whom Sarah bore to him—Isaac. Then Abraham circumcised his son Isaac when he was eight days old, as God had commanded him. Now Abraham was one hundred years old when his son Isaac was born to him. And Sarah said, "God has made me laugh, and all who hear will laugh with me." She also said, "Who would have said to Abraham that Sarah would nurse children? For I have borne him a son in his old age."* (Genesis 21:1-7)

Through the birth of their miracle baby, Abraham and Sarah learned five truths about God—the same truths that will enable you to make an indelible mark on the world.

What He Said He Would Do

In a panic, a young husband called the hospital. "I'm bringing my wife in right now," he almost shouted. "This is Harold Smith. She's about to have a baby!"

"Calm down," said the nurse. "Is this her first baby?"

After a long pause, Harold replied, "No, dummy. This is her husband."

Panic makes life hard. But when you're counting on an absolutely reliable God, you don't have to panic. You can stay calm and rest assured that whatever He has promised you, He'll fulfill. You can always rely on Him.

In Genesis 21:1, two phrases perfectly describe why we can rely on God: "as He had said" and "as He had spoken." Exactly as He said, God fulfilled His promise to Sarah about having a son. And just as He had spoken, He did it in a way only He could pull off.

For twenty-five years, God gave Abraham promise after promise that he would have a son. "I'm going to make you a great nation," God told him in chapter 12. In chapter 13, God insisted, "Your descendants will be as the dust of the Earth." In chapter 15, God said, "Abraham, go look at the stars. So shall your descendants be." Two chapters later, He said, "My covenant will be with you and with your descendants forever. And Sarah, your wife, will conceive and bear you a son." And then one year before the events in chapter 21, God showed up at Abraham's tent and said, "I'll be coming back one year from now, and at that time Sarah is going to have a son" (see Genesis 18). That's a lot of promises. And God kept every one of them.

Making promises will get you friends—but keeping promises will keep your friends. That's why God has the perfect friendship record. He is utterly and totally reliable. And that's the point of this first verse. *"And the LORD visited Sarah as He had said, and the LORD did for Sarah as He had spoken"* (Genesis 21:1). God did exactly what He said He would do. That's the essence of integrity. God said it and it happened.

Do you know what I most love about the story of Abraham and Sarah? Even though their sins complicated God's plan, God remained faithful and completely reliable—He kept His promises. Their foolishness couldn't trump His wisdom. Their story reminds us that God keeps His promises—whether we believe those promises or not. When Abraham and Sarah screwed up, God didn't say, "I've had it with you folks! I'm tired of this sin. I quit." No, He kept His promise.

God remains faithful even when we're far from it. Paul wrote, *"If we are faithless, He remains faithful; He cannot deny Himself"* (2 Timothy 2:13). God is reliable. You can take God's promises to the bank. You can count on them. You can trust them.

But do you?

The Bible contains 31,173 verses: about 23,000 in the Old Testament and 8,000 in the New. When we take only the promises God made, we come up with a grand total of 7,487 biblical promises. That's enough to live on, isn't it?

But what do you do with them? What do you do with all those grand promises of Almighty God? Some of us underline them. That's good. Some of us even go a step further and memorize them. That's even better. But the best is to live on them. To lean completely and count on them. To bank on them.

Years ago when the Blackfoot Indians controlled a large area of Alberta, Canada, Chief Crowfoot allowed the Canadian Pacific Railroad to place its tracks across Indian country, all the way from Medicine Hat to Calgary. In exchange for the use of Indian land, the railroad gave Crowfoot a lifetime pass. He could get on the railroad anytime he wanted and ride it anywhere he wanted to go. Guess what the chief did with that lifetime railroad pass. He put it in a little leather pouch and wore it around his neck. Never once did he use it.[2]

Isn't this just like some of us? We have hundreds of God's promises, but all we do is put them on plaques and stick them in cards and get nice leather pouches for our Bibles to carry them around. But God means for us to live on His promises. We can rely completely on them because the God who gives them is totally reliable. He did for Abraham and Sarah exactly what He said He'd do, and He'll do for you exactly what He says He will do.

You can count on it.

Just in Time

Savages in the jungles of South America once captured an explorer. As they danced around him, getting ready to feast on his soon-to-be-dead body, he tried to think of some way to escape. Finally he decided to awe them with magic, so he pulled a cigarette lighter out of his pocket and waved it around.

"I am a fire maker," he exclaimed, and with one flick of his thumb, the little lighter burst into flames. The savages fell back in amazement. "Magic," he said.

The chief watched the whole thing and replied, "It sure is! It's the only time we've ever seen a lighter work the first time."

Lighters aren't always dependable—but God is. You never have to worry about God showing up late. He's always on time.

When did Sarah bear her son, Isaac? The Bible says, *"Sarah conceived and bore Abraham a son in his old age,* at the set time of which God had spoken to him" (Genesis 21:2, emphasis mine). Back in chapter 18 God said, "Abraham, I'll return at the appointed time, and on that date—not before, and not afterward—you and Sarah are going to have this child." (See Genesis 18:10.)

Sometimes we have to wait long and hard for God to fulfill His promises. Abraham and Sarah had to wait for twenty-five years. The writer of Hebrews said to *"imitate those who through faith and patience inherit the promises"* (Hebrews 6:12).

Although God gave us His promises, we need to add something to them. We need faith and patience. And we don't like that second one, do we? I trust God, but I want Him to give me patience now. I want the promise now. We may wait for what seems a long time, but you know what?

God is never late. And He's never early. God is never behind the times or ahead of the times. He's always right on time.

God promised that Israel would remain in Egypt four hundred years and guess how many years they were there? Four hundred. God promised Israel would remain in captivity in Babylon for seventy years—and they were captive in Babylon for seventy years. God promised that the Messiah would show up in Jerusalem exactly 173,880 days after a king issued a commandment to restore and rebuild the city—exactly 173,880 days—and guess what day Jesus rode into Jerusalem on a donkey? On the 173,880th day—not the 173,881st. Not the 173,879th. Jesus arrived exactly on time.

Paul wrote, *"But when the fullness of the time had come, God sent forth His son, born of a woman, born under the law"* (Galatians 4:4). That's how Jesus operated during His whole earthly ministry. He repeatedly said things like: "It's not yet my time;" "The time has not yet come;" "Now is your time, but not my time." He operated with an impeccable sense of timing. Even when it looked like He had arrived late—remember when He showed up in Bethany four days after his friend Lazarus died?—it turned out that He was on the dot, after all.

God will always keep His appointments with you—even if you don't see anything happening right now. Perhaps you've been praying and waiting a long time, and you feel tempted to give up. Don't! God will keep His appointment with you.

"But when? Why isn't anything happening?"

Because it's not time yet. But at the right time—He'll be there.

Before I had a car my father used to pick me up after school. He had a notorious reputation for being late. All my friends knew that I would be the last kid standing out in front of the school, waiting to get picked up. My dad was a busy man.

You may feel as though your relationship with God is just like that. It seems like He's notoriously late, especially regarding the things you feel most passionate about. He could've done this so long ago. What's He waiting for?

Peter said, *"The Lord is not slack concerning His promise, as some count slackness"* (2 Peter 3:9). Nope—God is always right on time.

Charles Spurgeon wrote, "There are no loose threads in the providence of God. No stitches are dropped. No events are left to chance. The great clock of the universe keeps good time, and the whole machinery of providence moves with unerring punctuality."

Years ago in Scotland, the Clark family had a dream to move to the United States of America—a big task, because the Clarks had nine kids. Mr. Clark needed to save up enough money and get all the passports and tickets and everything else he needed to move eleven people from Scotland to America. He saved, worked hard, and planned. Finally, the day came when he had saved all the cash he needed. He bought passports, made reservations on a brand-new ocean liner, and got his family ready to go.

Seven days before setting off from Liverpool, England, a dog bit his youngest son. The doctor sewed up the cut, but because they feared rabies the whole family was quarantined for two weeks. They missed their ship.

Mr. Clark was angry—angry at God, angry at his boy, angry at the dog—until five days after the ship sailed. Then he got the news that the Titanic, the "unsinkable" ocean liner on which they intended to sail, had sunk—1,517 lives were lost. When Mr. Clark heard the news, he hugged his son, hugged the dog, and thanked God for saving the Clark family just in time.[3]

That delay? It may actually be an appointment with destiny.

Loud and Clear

NASA launched a rocket to the moon with two pigs and a stunning blonde named Kiki on board. When the rocket passed the stratosphere, the first stage dropped off and mission control contacted the spacecraft.

"Houston here, Pig One. Pig One, do you read? Over."

"Oink, oink. Pig One here. Read you loud and clear."

"Pig One, do you still remember your instructions?"

"Yes. When we get to the moon, I press the red button to initiate the moon landing. Over."

"That is correct. Over and out."

Some time later, the booster stage separated from the rocket.

"Hello, Pig Two? Come in, please."

"Oink, oink. Pig Two here. Read you loud and clear."

"Pig Two, do you remember your instructions?"

"Yes. When we've landed on the moon and are ready to leave, I press the green button to initiate the launch program."

"That is correct, Pig Two. Over and out."

An hour later, when the rocket achieved its correct speed, the final stage dropped off.

"Houston here. Kiki, come in. Kiki, do you read us?"

"Kiki here, reading you loud and clear."

"Kiki, do you remember your instructions?"

"Yes. I feed the two pigs and keep my hands off any buttons."[4]

We need to know who should initiate and who should respond. In our relationship with the Lord, God initiates and man responds. Abraham named his infant son Isaac because God suggested the naming; Abraham simply obeyed God's instructions. (See Genesis 21:3.) Because God acted in faithfulness, He expected Abraham to act in obedience. God initiated; Abraham responded.

Eight days after Isaac's birth, Abraham circumcised his son. Why? Because it was God's command. (See Genesis 17:12.) God initiated in grace; Abraham responded in faith. What a great dad! From the beginning, he put his son on the right spiritual track. He gave him the outward mark that identified him as one of God's covenant people.

When God initiates something by giving us a promise, we should respond to His overture with obedience. *"We love Him because He first loved us"* (1 John 4:19). He promises (because He loves us), and we obey (because we love Him).

A lot of times we try to bargain with God: "Well, God, if you save me from this, I promise to _____" (fill in the blank).

Two sailors stranded in a raft out in the sea thought, *We're dead men.* For days they saw no one. And so one sailor prayed, "God, I'm sorry. I've led a worthless life. I haven't paid attention to my kids. I haven't been kind to my wife. But I promise, Lord, if you save me I'll ..." At that moment the second sailor said, "Hold it. I see land!" In other words, "Whatever you were going to promise God, you don't have to promise anymore, because we're okay."

Most of the time that's totally wrong. Finding land should prompt devotion, not avoidance. Abraham got it right. God's faithfulness in fulfilling His promise prompted Abraham's fruitfulness in obeying his God. The Lord initiated, and Abraham responded. That's the kind of response that sets us up to make an indelible mark on the world.

It's a Miracle

Thirteen ministers boarded an airplane and traveled together from the West Coast to New York City. Along the way the plane encountered some turbulence from a big storm and the engines started acting up. The plane bounced up and down, shuddered, and trembled.

One minister grabbed the attention of a flight attendant heading toward the cockpit and said to her, "Hey, you tell the pilot it's going to be all right. He's got thirteen ministers on his airplane."

She dutifully conveyed the message and when she returned a few minutes later, the minister asked her, "Did you give him the message?"

She smiled and said, "Yeah, I told him. He says he's happy to have thirteen ministers on his airplane, but he'd rather have four good engines."

Unlike airplane engines, God will never let you down. He is fully capable of fulfilling every promise He makes. Abraham knew this. And that's why Paul testified that Abraham was fully convinced that what God promised, He was also able to perform. (See Romans 4:21.)

God is capable.

Think about Abraham's situation for a moment. God didn't fulfill His promise to give Abraham and Sarah a son until he became a centenarian and she had reached her nineties. On a human level, keeping such a promise would be impossible. So God performed something humanly impossible. He worked a miracle. That's the whole point of the descriptions found in Romans 4:19 and Hebrews 11:12—Abraham was "as good as dead." By using an elderly man with a body as good as dead, God brought forth a people "as many as the stars of the sky in multitude."

Miracles aren't everyday occurrences, but we have a tendency to "over-naturalize" the miraculous. I hear it all the time.

"Oh, a baby was born. What a little miracle!" No, it's not.

"The sunrise is a miracle." Nope.

"Finding a parking space at Christmastime is miraculous." No, it's providence.

We shouldn't say "miracle" when we're describing wonderful, but everyday, things. None of them are miracles in the biblical sense. Saint Augustine was right when he said, "The daily miracles of God grow cheap through repetition."

But the birth of Isaac was a miracle because something like it doesn't happen every day. When did you last hear about a ninety-year-old woman having a kid with her hundred-year-old husband? Webster's Dictionary defines a miracle as "an extraordinary event manifesting divine intervention in human affairs."

We need to know that the God we serve is capable. He can do anything. He can even perform miracles. The laws of nature don't imprison God; He created them and upholds them and can always supersede them. If we need a miracle, He can give it to us—no problem.

Our technological age has learned to override some natural laws, but only by bringing into play stronger natural laws. For example, the law of gravity says, "You're going to stay grounded on this Earth." But what happens when you board a 747, along with hundreds of other passengers and forty-five-thousand pounds of luggage? According to Isaac Newton and the universal law of gravity, what are the odds that such a weighty thing will get up in the air? It's earthbound—but the laws of aerodynamics allow that huge, heavy plane to glide across the sky from one part of the world to another. We have learned to override some natural laws by tapping into other natural laws.

But God doesn't need to use one law to overcome another one. God can do what He wants whenever He wants. What looks like a miracle to us is nothing unusual or difficult for Him. It's all the same to God, whether He's upholding "natural laws" or superseding them through "miracles."

From our perspective, the birth of Isaac was a miracle. The New Testament says, *"By faith Sarah herself also received strength to conceive seed, and she bore a child when she was past the age"* (Hebrews 11:11). At the age of ninety, how did Sarah even survive the trauma of childbirth? The Bible says that she "received strength to conceive." She benefited from a supernatural event. (By the way, it was a double miracle—she not only had a child; she also nursed the child.)

Are you in a tough marital situation? Did the doctor call about the cancer? Have you lost your job? Are you depressed? Since God is utterly capable, He has the strength and the ability to take care of anything that troubles you. I'm not saying that He will immediately heal you or take care of everything tomorrow—but He can if He chooses.

Like Abraham, you need to focus on the capability of God. You may be at the end of your resources, but God has a limitless supply of resources that He wants to make available to you.

The prophet Jeremiah took God's question in Genesis 18:14 (*"Is anything too hard for the LORD?"*) and turned it into an emphatic statement of faith. He prayed: *"Ah, Lord GOD! Behold, You have made the heavens and the earth by Your great power and outstretched arm. There is nothing too hard for You"* (Jeremiah 32:17).

When you love and serve a God with that kind of capability, why spend your time worrying? Still—most of us worry anyway. But then we listen to Jesus tell His disciples, *"The things which are impossible with men are possible with God"* (Luke 18:27).

So relax. God is capable.

Making You Laugh

Did you know that the average child laughs four hundred times every day, but the average adult laughs only fifteen times a day?[5]

When did we stop laughing?

A lot of us try to blame God. "God made me angry." "God made me grumpy." "God made me serious." A writer in *Christianity Today* said, "Some people think it's hard to be a Christian and to laugh, but I think it's the other way around. God writes a lot of comedy—it's just that he has so many bad actors."[6] I agree. We have too many bad actors in the kingdom.

Laughter has so many physical and mental benefits. Laughing produces hormones that facilitate healing, reduce inflammation, and enhance relaxation. Laughing increases the heart rate, raises blood pressure, speeds up breathing, and increases oxygen consumption. Then the heart rate slows down, the blood pressure drops, and the muscles relax. Laughter aids in digestion. Laughter also can raise pain tolerance, even with obstetrical patients.[7]

Of course, the Bible knows all of that. Some three thousand years ago, Solomon wrote, *"A merry heart does good, like medicine, but a broken spirit dries the bones"* (Proverbs 17:22).

But too many people connect Christianity with the exact opposite.

"Oh, you're a Christian. I'm so sorry. You must be very sad. You must have no life at all. You had nowhere else to turn. You were at the end of your rope." Some of us do come to Christ when we reach the end of our rope, but

He leaves us with joy, not sadness. Genuine Christianity doesn't sap the flavor from life—it pumps zest into it.

We know that Isaac brought laughter into the home of Abraham and Sarah. His very name means "laughter." Picture this: one day Sarah meets a new neighbor and introduces her boy.

"This is my son," she says.

"What's his name?"

"Laughter," Sarah replies with a big grin.

"Really? Tell me about it."

"I laughed when God told me I was going to have him. I said, 'God, have you looked at me lately? Have you looked at my husband lately?'"

Here's Isaac, the miracle child—he made everyone laugh. Such joy! Such delight! Such happiness! How outlandish is that? The only appropriate response is laughter. God is so good! What else can you do but laugh?

Two Scriptures come to mind as I ponder the miraculous experience of this elderly couple: *"Hope deferred makes the heart sick, but when the desire comes, it is a tree of life"* (Proverbs 13:12). Abraham and Sarah experienced both ends of that proverb.

The second is from Psalm 30. As David dedicated his house, he reflected on the staggering goodness of God: *"You have turned for me my mourning into dancing; You have loosed my sackcloth and girded me with gladness"* (Psalm 30:11, NASB).

Does God make you laugh?

Theologian Helmut Thielicke once wrote something very profound: "Should we not see that lines of laughter about the eyes are just as much marks of faith as are our lines of care and seriousness? Is it only earnestness that is to be baptized? Is laughter pagan? We have already allowed too much that is good to be lost to the church."

One day a motorist got pulled over for speeding. The police officer asked the driver for his license and registration, and then walked back to his patrol car to check out the information. After a few moments the policeman returned to the driver to give him a citation. Hoping for some leniency, the speeder said with a smile, "Officer, did you notice my birthday was yesterday?"

The police officer smiled back and said, "Why, yes, I did. Because that's when your license expired." The man got two tickets instead of one.

How's that for bounty? Sometimes we receive a very unpleasant sort.

But you don't have to worry about God dropping that sort of unpleasant bounty on you. He loves to do good to His children. So God lavished upon Abraham and Sarah blessing after blessing—not just promise after promise, but blessing after blessing after blessing. God gave them land. Wealth. Hundreds of servants. And finally, He gave them a son in their old age. God turned a retirement home into a maternity ward—that's bounty!

Penguins

A girl went to a computer dating service with several specific qualities in mind for a potential mate. "I want somebody short who likes formal attire and who loves water sports," she declared.

The computer sent her a penguin.

You may think you know what you want and need, but beware of ordering up penguins. Leave the details in God's hands. He really does know exactly what you need—and what will make you laugh after you get it.

I hope you finish this book and decide to be more joyful. And decide to focus more on the greatness of God rather than on the magnitude of your problems. After all, God is reliable. God is punctual. God initiates. God is capable. God is bountiful. And if all that is true (and it is), and you know Him (I hope you do), then you can decide right now to act on the words of Nehemiah as he spoke to the people of Jerusalem rebuilding the wall around their ruined city: *"Do not sorrow, for the joy of the LORD is your strength"* (Nehemiah 8:10).

MEDITATING ⬤N THE MARK

In this chapter we learned that God provided Abraham and his family with abundant joy and blessings—including laughter. The story of Abraham and Sarah reveal five characteristics of God to us. He is reliable, punctual, initial, capable, and bountiful.

Reliable. God promised Abraham and Sarah a son and, even though their sins complicated God's plan, He was still faithful and reliable to keep His promise. What do you do with God's promises?

Punctual. Abraham waited twenty-five years before God's promise to him was fulfilled. The Lord's timing is always exactly on time. How faithful and patient are you when it comes to waiting on Him? Remind yourself of His awesome timing.

Initial. Remember that God acted in faithfulness and expected Abraham to act in obedience. Do you find yourself bargaining with God more than responding to Him?

Capable. Sarah was over ninety years old when she gave birth to Isaac and nursed him. God can do anything. Are you focusing on the capability of God and the wonder of His miracles?

Bountiful. Abraham and Sarah were lavished with blessings. How often do you count the blessings in your life?

MODELING THE MASTER'S MARK

Reliable. Acts 2:39: *"For the promise is to you and to your children, and to all who are afar off, as many as the Lord our God will call."*

Punctual. Psalm 27:14: *"Wait on the LORD; be of good courage, and He shall strengthen your heart; wait, I say, on the LORD!"*

Initial. John 14:15: *"If you love Me, keep My commandments."*

Capable. Luke 1:37: *"For with God nothing will be impossible."*

Bountiful. Galatians 3:14: *"That the blessing of Abraham might come upon the Gentiles in Christ Jesus, that we might receive the promise of the Spirit through faith."*

MAKING YOUR MARK

God will keep His promises if He makes them—regardless of your belief in those promises. Who have you promised something to? Fulfill that promise today.

Go Fish!

Sam made his living as a fisherman. One day the game warden noticed that Sam always seemed to bring in far more fish than any of his competitors. When they brought in three or four, Sam returned with his boat full of fish. So one afternoon the warden moseyed over to Sam's boat.

"What's your secret, Sam?" he asked. "How do you catch so many?"

"Warden," Sam replied, "come with me tomorrow morning and I'll show you how I do it."

So they went out early the next morning. With Sam's boat anchored in the middle of the lake, the warden watched as Sam took out a stick of dynamite, lit it, and tossed it in the air. The thunderous explosion shook the lake with such force that scores of dead fish surfaced. As you can imagine, the warden came unglued.

"Sam," he yelled. "I'm going to put you in jail and throw every fine in the book at you!"

Sam watched him for a few moments, grabbed another stick of dynamite, lit it, and then tossed it in the warden's lap.

"Warden," he said, "are you going to sit there all day complaining or are you going to fish?"

The warden had to make a decision—and in less than a second he moved from observer to participant.

That's what Abraham's life is trying to tell you. God is calling you to make a decision about your life. Oh, you can complain about your life: "It's mediocre. It's going nowhere. What's the point?" Or you can decide—with God's help—to change things. And the first step is to invite Christ into your "boat"—your life.

You may not decide to ask the Captain to board your ship. "Been baptized," you might say. "Been dedicated." "Been confirmed." Fine. But if you respond like that, then you've made your decision. You have told God, "No, I don't want You in control." You will have to live with that decision and die with it.

Just make sure you know the stakes.

A chaplain joined the armed services during wartime. Soldiers gathered around him and asked, "Sir, do you believe in hell?"

"No, I don't," he replied.

One soldier responded, "Then would you please resign?"

"Why should I resign?" the chaplain asked, offended.

"Well, if there's no hell, then we don't need you," the soldier answered. "But if there is a hell, then we don't need you to lead us astray."

The Captain invites you to climb aboard His vessel.

A hundred or so years ago, during the heyday of homesteading, one group on its way west moved slowly across the plains in covered wagons. Suddenly someone noticed smoke rising on the horizon, many miles wide— and moving toward the wagon train at a tremendous rate of speed. "A brush fire!" the men screamed. "We're doomed!" they wailed.

One man kept his wits about him and decided to light his own fire. He burned all of the grass around the wagons, the horses, and the people. As the big brush fire approached, it looked terrifying. Most of the homesteaders were sure they were about to die.

But the man who lit the fire said, "You can relax. The flames can't reach us here. We're standing where the fire's already been."

If you have placed your faith in Christ, then you're standing where the fire has already been. If you've never committed your life to Christ, then you're standing directly in the path of the biggest fire you have never seen.

Make the best decision you can. Make sure you know the stakes. And then answer the question: are you going to complain all day—or are you going to fish?

If you have not already accepted Jesus Christ as your Lord and personal Savior, do it now. Please don't wait. With a sincere and repentant heart, simply pray:

> **Father, I know I am a sinner. I repent of my sin, and turn away from it. I turn to Jesus. I believe that Jesus died on the Cross and rose again, saving all who believe in Him. Fill me with your Spirit and come into my life. Transform me. Make me into a new creation.**
>
> **I pray this in Jesus' name.**

If you prayed this prayer, please contact Calvary of Albuquerque at (505) 344-0880.

ENDNOTES

Chapter Three

1   www.en.wikipedia.org/wiki/Liebeck v._McDonald's_Restaurants

2   www.goodreads.com/.../611609.Wearing_of_This_Garment_Does_Not_Enable_You_to_Fly_101_Real_Dumb_Warning_Labels

3   http://en.wikipedia.org/wiki/Isaac_Newton

Chapter Four

1   http://www.telegraph.co.uk/culture/film/3671166/Revisiting-the-riddle-of-Baker-Street.html

Chapter Five

1   www.cfdevotionals.org/studies

2   http://sectofentrance.homestead.com/satanism4.html

3   http://www.greenspun.com/bboard/q-and-a-fetch-msg.tcl?msg_id=00CREt

4   "I'd Rather Have Jesus" George Beverly Shea.

5   http://www.bookfinder.com/dir/i/Integrity-Character_from_the_Inside_Out/0877886342/

Chapter Six

1   Elisabeth Elliot, 1995, *Keep A Quiet Heart* (Servant Publications, Ann Arbor Michigan). She says the story is a first-person account given to her from Jessica Foltz of Princeton, Minnesota. http://dalesdesigns.net/ant_lens.htm

2   www.wisc.edu/

3   http://famouspoetsandpoems.com/poets/shel_silverstein/
poems/14819

Chapter Seven

1   http://www.google.com/search?q=You+can+make+the+cl
ock+strike+before+the+hour+by+putting+your+hand+on
+it%2C+but+it+will+strike+wrong.+You+can+tear+the+r
osebud+open+before+its+time%2C+but+you+will+mar+
its+beauty.+You+may+spoil+many+gifts+of+blessing+tha
t+God+is+preparing+for+you+because+of+your+own+ea
ger+haste&ie=utf-8&oe=utf-8&aq=t&rls=org.mozilla:en-
US:official&client=firefox-a

Chapter Eight

1   http://www.fhs64.com/fhsold/perks.htm

2   http://www.sermonillustrations.com/a-z/a/age.htm

3   www.dropzone.com/news/General/more3.html

Chapter Nine

1   *The Tale of the Tardy Oxcart*, Charles R. Swindoll, Word
Publishing, Nashville, 1998, p 372.

2   http://www.uss-bennington.org/hu-training-captmessage.html

3   Source unknown

4   http://www.slkcofc.org/11-19-06.pdf

Chapter Ten

1   http://www.humorbin.com/showitem.asp?item=34

2   *Cast of Characters By Max Lucado*, Max Lucado, B.A., M.A.

3   Bob Jones, Sr. http://www.minresctr.org/resources/quotes.htm

4   http://www.inspirationtruth.com/?page_id=3

5   http://legacy.pastors.com/RWMT/article.asp?ID=182&ArtID=
7704&printerfriendly=1

Chapter Eleven

1 http://www.google.com/search?q=on+the+first+day%2C+
   God+created+the+cow&ie=utf-8&oe=utf-8&aq=t&rls=org.
   mozilla:en-US:official&client=firefox-a

2 www.lakesfree.org/Sermons/SermonPDF/05-04-08sermon.pdf

3 www.unm.edu

4 www.bib-arch.org/e-features/sodom-and-gomorrah.asp

5 www.sermonillustrations.com/a-z/e/evil.htm

Chapter Twelve

1 http://www.shimen.org/web/resource/yingyu/show.
   aspx?id=68&cid=25

2 http://www.mhs.mb.ca/docs/pageant/05/chiefcrowfoot.shtml

3 http://titanic3.tripod.com/stories.html

4 http://miamijokes.com/node/958

5 http://www.anvari.org/fun/Truth/Useless_Facts.html

6 http://en.wikipedia.org/wiki/Garrison_Keillor

7 http://www.helpguide.org/life/humor_laughter_health.htmw